THE
UNIVERSAL
STANDARD
OF
LOVE

THE TRUTHS AND PRINCIPLES OF
TRUE LOVE

B.J. JERREMY

J. SKYLIMIT
PUBLISHING

A J. SKYLIMIT PUBLISHING BOOK

THE UNIVERSAL STANDARD OF LOVE: The Truths and Principles of True Love.

Produced in the United States of America.

ISBN-10: 0983933502
ISBN-13: 978-0-9839335-0-2

Published by
J. Skylimit Publishing
P.O. Box 649
South Pasadena, California 91031

Dedicated to all of humanity

Truth is a passage to enlightenment and happiness.
Only in absolute truth and knowledge are we equipped
to live in accordance with the natural laws of creation.
When love is light, why live in darkness.
We must live in the light of love!

CONTENTS

THE UNIVERSAL STANDARD OF LOVE

PREFACE

IN THE NAME OF LOVE

Love is one of the most powerful words used by humans. It is a word so strong and powerful that it can conjure up a myriad of feelings, emotions, and thoughts in the minds of the masses. Throughout the history of humanity as we know it, humans have used it as a rationale to wage war against each other, as some go to war in the name of love. In the same light, it has also been used as a medium to make peace between people. This illustrates the profound power of the word "love."

It is safe to say that since the genesis of humanity this word and its profound power has perplexed and befuddled human beings. Although there are various words used to express this feeling due to the many different languages on earth, it remains a fact that the feelings and emotions it can elicit are universally beyond bounds. It is therefore only logical to surmise that any misunderstanding or misinformation on the concept and principles of love will ultimately plunge many individuals into great depths of unconscious actions and misguided behavior.

In light of the foregoing, these questions and many more resonate in the minds of the masses – young and old alike: What is the meaning of love and what is its purpose? Should love hurt? What are some of the principles that denote true love? Is love truly blind? Where and how do I find true love? Can love bring me happiness?

As in a painting that is incomplete, it is difficult, if not impossible, to formulate the true message of the artist. Such applies to the many sectors and groups that provide limited, distorted, or misleading answers to some of these questions. However, before we can accurately answer these questions, it is imperative that we first ask ourselves this important question: What do we really know about love?

The erudition of humans shrouded in numerous scientific studies does nothing to provide sufficient or logical answers to the many questions that boggle the minds of so many. That should come as no surprise, as it is inconceivable that studies and concepts developed by the human brain will have the absolute answers. That is because such studies are strongly based on researchable and quantifiable earthly phenomena. Therefore, it is only logical that such studies will be limited in trying to provide sufficient answers to that which is not solely of the material world.

Most individuals base their understanding of love on religious studies and teachings passed down for generations. However, the many religious sects only provide a limited picture on this subject. Some of the teachings provided seem to create more conundrums and confusion in the minds of earnest seekers and follower as a result of the many inconsistencies. These inconsistencies arise due to the gross distortions and misinterpretations to the meaning of some of the teachings, proverbs, and parables about love entailed in the many scriptures they read.

Further along this line, the romanticized images and messages promulgated in popular culture only serve to further confuse the masses. The messages sent out through the various entertainment mediums have reduced the concept of love to a mundane and almost meaningless utterance. As a result of this, many do not even know the meaning of the words they utter, but do so just to belong to the crowd.

What is more appalling is the fact that the messages sent out to the masses are done by the so-called "cream of the society," who know little, if anything, about the concept and principles of true love. The messages sent out by these persons tend to focus greatly on the acts perceived to be performed to those they claim to love, as can be seen in the many movies, books, and songs about love.

Most of what is seen, read, or sung about are the selfish attempts to satisfy the physical desires of individuals under the disguise of love. In so doing, unfortunately, they forget or comfortably bypass the important elements such as their thoughts, words, actions, and behavior towards those they claim to love. The by-product of all this only further creates a world with a multiplicity of persons who are confused about the meaning and principles of true love.

In view of all this, to an independent observer, it is very clear and apparent that there are many inconsistencies, misconceptions, and distorted ideologies about love that are influenced by the popular cultures of the world. As it is, some have taken conventional beliefs to be the truth. The most noteworthy of all is the perplexing notion that *"Love is blind."* All around the world, despite the fact that the perceptions of love differ due to cultural differences, there is an overwhelming number of persons who ascribe to the notion that love is blind. Why is such the case?

It is understood that this phrase is not meant to be taken solely at face value, as the connotations and applications vary; nonetheless, on the surface, and even with further analysis, this statement sounds ridiculous at best. The fact that such a saying remains a prevailing sentiment in the minds of the masses brings one to a state of amazement as to how such can be. In light of that, we should all ask ourselves a pertinent question: How do we explain that something so sacred is devoid of sight?

A possible explanation that some might give is that love is said to be blind because when "in love" one is blindly oblivious to all factors – especially the negative factors they perceive. This line of thinking clearly explains why so many suffer under the "guise of love." One of the reasons why the belief that love is blind is so powerful and greatly misleading is that it seems to justify the notion that one can love those who are hurtful, evil, or destructive forces to humanity. In the name of love, some believe that the "blindness of love" means that they must be blind to the negativity that is woefully apparent in others. As it is, it is all too clear that the belief that love is blind is only a figment of the imagination, and even worse, it is a conscious deception of one's mind, which is overtly propagated to help many individuals justify the persistence in their various relationships in which there are obvious signs of an absence of true love. That in turn has propelled so many persons into numerous unpropitious experiences.

To obviate ourselves from heeding to misguided fables, we must consciously seek the truths of living for ourselves. On account of that, many might wonder where to go for the answers. Well, the answers lie within each and every conscious human being. That is simply saying that the answers to the many questions that boggle the minds of so many are inherent within each and every individual. All we have to do is consciously look deep within ourselves. Only by seeking earnestly do the answers become apparent. However, to do this effectively, those who truly seek must rid themselves of old and archaic concepts and beliefs that only serve to blind and misdirect them from the truth.

The deception and misdirection of so many come as a result of trying to find the answers solely in the material world. There is no mistaking that those who lack true knowledge on this subject only serve to further mislead the many followers who listen attentively to their messages. The true answers to the great questions in creation that so many have pondered about do not lie solely in the material world, as the material world is largely defined and characterized by what we can see, hear, and touch. The truth is felt! It is that which we feel at the core of our Being.

It is therefore exhorted that all individuals search deep enough. They must consciously strive to become spiritually in tune with themselves. Only then will the answers become apparent to all those who seek with humility. It is impossible to talk about true love without spelling out the importance of a spiritual foundation and understanding. Only in doing so is the picture whole.

Although we live in a material world, it is undeniable that we are spiritual beings. Therefore, the true understanding of love which we experience in the material realm – the physical world – must also be balanced with that which emanates from the spirit of humans – the immaterial factors. A one-sided view or understanding is greatly misleading and incomplete; as it is bound to propel many individuals into practices that stem from misguided beliefs and ideologies. And that can only lead to more suffering and confusion.

The idea of love is neither difficult to understand nor is it complicated. As a result of gross misinformation and ill-practices, many choose to make it that way. The reason so many are puzzled by the concept of love is because the masses are not knowledgeable about its principles; or in some cases, they are well aware of these principles but consciously choose to ignore them. Many men and women have been misled to expect acts and deeds that do not fall under the principles of true love, and in so doing, they lower their standards so as to accommodate mediocrity in family members, friends, and potential partners. As it is, the belief that love is blind is the number one reason why so many individuals remain in the trenches of gross suffering in the name of love. That should not be the case!

Now, in order to break many individuals out of the chains of love shackles and entrapments, it is important to provide a clear message that frees the minds of those who ascribe to misguided and archaic notions that do them no good. It is important to provide seeds that will germinate into conscious thoughts. In order for this new consciousness to seep in, we must open the doors of our minds to a new mindset. This will be a mindset of total liberation. This new mindset will come with the full recognition and awareness of what love was meant to be for humankind. On that account, it is essential to spell out "The Universal Standard of Love" for all to see.

THE PURPOSE OF THIS WORK

This work brings a seldom told message of love to the masses. It will serve in addressing some of the fallacies, myths, and misnomers that pertain to the matters of love. The writing provided in this book is not intended to continuously mislead the masses by presenting a set of silly rules, strategies, tactics, or tricks on how to falsely attain love. Rather, it serves to openly pronounce the universal truths and key principles of love which are unchangeable in creation. Also, more importantly, this work addresses how we can apply these principles in our lives for a balanced and fulfilling earthly existence.

This work will also serve in presenting a balanced view of love, as it delves deep into some of the questions that have plagued humanity since the beginning of our consciousness. This message is provided with the conscious consideration that although there are cultural differences in the understanding of love, the truths and principles of love – as well as other forces at play in creation – stand true notwithstanding any personal or cultural differences, because they are in accordance with the natural laws of creation.

The reason for presenting this work to the world is as a result of the great urging from within me to help awaken humankind to the inherent truths in creation. In observing the state of our world, it has become very clear that this message must be given to humanity. Knowing these principles and consciously living by them in totality will ultimately set each person free of love burdens. It is my fervent hope that those who seek the truths of love will derive from this work that which will help guide them in making better life decisions.

The principles presented are all in strict alignment with the natural laws of creation; therefore, I strongly believe that each reader will gain something valuable from them. Nothing presented is beyond the scope of human understanding, for it is given in a very simple way. The words and messages are concise and direct. It is written in a way that it creates no allowance for vagueness, ambiguity, or misinterpretations. Though forceful at times, it is not meant to create resistance or dissension. Rather, presented with pure intentions, it is meant to open the eyes and ears of many to a message they have not seen or heard about love. It is also important to note that nothing presented is set-in-stone or provided as a mandate to the masses on how to live their lives. I simply lay down the truths and principles of love for all to see.

In relaying this message, I consciously highlighted some important key notes to make it easier for readers to grasp the information. Also, occasionally, at certain points, I will ask readers to pause and cogitate about a point presented. In doing so, they will be able to absorb the message, and hopefully they will get the essence of what is being said.

Now, I must say that this work is not for those who look for "quick-fix prescriptions" without conscious conviction in their actions. It is not for those who seek tricks or strategies to circumvent the natural laws of creation in an attempt to falsely attain love; nor is it for those who are impervious to change because they are stuck in dogmatic agendas prescribed by another without seeking out the truths for themselves. This work is meant to reaffirm the truth in those who diligently search for answers and knowledge that can propel them to a heightened state of consciousness. It is meant to spark the light of consciousness in all human beings – the consciousness of love. It is my fervent hope that those who come across this work will find within it that which will take them to greater heights.

I am sure that this work might not wholly appeal to certain readers, as there might be certain persons who object at impulse or vigorously attempt to impugn the principles and concepts of discussion entailed in this work. To these persons, it must be said that in order to fully grasp the information that will be presented, it is advised that they read this work in its entirety, and as they do so, they must rid themselves of impulsive opposition to the points presented. In doing so, they open themselves, thus unclogging their minds so as to gain full understanding of the message within.

We all have the truths and answers within us! What differentiates the so-called enlightened persons from the masses is not the fact that they are inherently superior or that they possess esoteric knowledge which is naturally unavailable to everyone else. Rather, it is due to the fact that they made a conscious decision to apply the learned principles in their lives, whilst some others decide to remain in the abyss of misdirection by following distorted teachings or the messages promulgated in popular culture, which are superficial at best. *One can only lead a thirsty group to the stream, what each member of the group does on arrival is totally dependent on the drive to quench his or her thirst.*

Before we delve straight into this topic, it is important to make note that this work strictly illustrates my innate knowledge and observations on this matter. Therefore, it should not be misconstrued as that of a scholar with intentions to lecture or garner followers. This work has no religious, scientific, or philosophical affiliations; nor does it attempt to disperse any form of religion or philosophical thought. As such, it *must not* be tied to any schools of thought or philosophical programs. It simply speaks the truths which are apparent in creation, as can easily be observed by any conscious observer. Now, let us begin.

1

LOVE IN CREATION

What is love and what is its purpose in creation? This is the ultimate question. It is a question that has befuddled humanity since the beginning of time as we know it. In order to understand the concept of love and what denotes true love, it is important that we all have a basic understanding of the general definition of the word.

The word "love" is commonly defined simply as a *feeling of strong affection*. Along this line, it is also important to note that the word "affection" is defined as a *fond feeling*. Therefore, we can safely surmise that a more encompassing definition of love is: A strong feeling of fondness towards someone or something. Now, on the surface, this definition might suffice. However, simply put, such a mundane definition does no justice to capture the real meaning and essence of true love, as it only scratches the surface of its deeper meaning. Unfortunately, the mundanity of the definition of love gives many individuals a very simple, naive, incomplete, and unsubstantiated gleam of the total picture. This is so as it focuses mainly on the mere physical, which is largely characterized by human *emotions and feelings*.

The simplicity of this definition makes it easy for the masses to conjure up misinterpretations on the subject. And as a result of this myopic view, the *idea of love* is now belittled to mean acts that thrive in direct opposition to the principles of true love in creation. To further compound the issue of looking at it from this simple extenuation, it is sad to say that the scientific and religious views also fall short in providing us with the complete truth. All the masses receive from these groups are *grains of truth* without the total picture; thereby leading many into false beliefs and wrong expectations about love. Now, in order to gain a thorough and more comprehensive understanding on this subject, it is imperative that we delve much deeper into the true meaning and nature of the word as well as its implications for humankind.

THE DEPENDENCE ON THE INTELLECT

In the search for answers, it is unfortunate that some individuals depend and operate solely with the intellect. They do this by focusing greatly on the workings of their brains. And in so doing, they block themselves to that which can easily be perceived without intellection. Most do this because they do not know that the intellect was only given to humans as a tool to help us navigate our earthly journey. It is not meant to be overworked and developed to a point of incapacity.

With the overwhelming dependence on the intellect, when individuals are faced with unascertainable quandaries, some boldly say, "If the intellect or brain cannot answer it, then it is unanswerable." This statement illustrates gross "intellectual arrogance" at its highest, for they perceive that they are the sole proprietors of knowledge and truth. Those who make such assertions *unknowingly* prove that such matters are imponderable solely by using the intellect – the brain's limited capacity. As such, it is easier to assume that they have no answers. However, the fact is that these queries deemed "unanswerable" are simply beyond the scope of human intellectual understanding.

In looking at the various categories of erudition developed by the human intellect – the sciences – for the answers, it becomes very apparent that they are limited in their scope of knowledge and understanding on matters that are not solely of the material world. This is evident when we look at the magnitude of new discoveries and addenda to what was previously accepted as an "established fact," of which there was unanimous consensus among so-called erudite scholars of its definitude as a fact. This should leave one to wonder what questions the sciences can truly answer, for the "truths" they proclaim are ever changing.

The fact that the human sciences define their findings based on extensive research as "new discoveries" does not alleviate the fact that these laws and principles have been in play since the inception of human consciousness. Sadly, it takes us time to discover them, and when we do, it is greatly publicized as a new invention or discovery. Although there are numerous examples to help illustrate this point, let us take a look at just one historic instance which pertains to the understanding of the "shape of the earth."

At some point in human history, there was the prominent belief and perception that the surface and shape of the earth was flat. Though there were some who opposed such a notion because it was practically illogical, this sentiment prevailed in the minds of many. The modern-day understanding of the true composition and shape of the earth leaves one to wonder why and how such a notion was prevalent at that time. This only serves to show how the limited capacity of human understanding can serve to distract us from that which is all too apparent when we do not consciously open our eyes to the truths around us.

As a consequence of this gross misconception, the so-called learned persons of the time wrongfully thought and proclaimed this message to the masses; and as a result, served to deceive them. It is easy to see that any ideas and calculations made under that premise were also wrong and misleading. The fact that the earth is spherical in shape has remained an unmistakable fact since the inception of human existence. The wrong assumptions of certain individuals will never change that inherent fact of nature. It only serves to throw many into a loop of misguided ideologies and beliefs. *If the basis is flawed, the whole will be wrong!*

This example and explanation was not made to dismiss or question the true intentions of the sciences. The sciences are very important to humans and our existence on this planet because they strive to provide answers to help humanity understand the forces at play in nature. However, we must realize that they are extremely limited in the scope of truths and knowledge they can provide in dealing with matters that are beyond material observations. This is because such matters are out of their jurisdiction since they verge on the abstract, and as such, are *beyond the physical plane* of human understanding through quantifiable and researchable means. Science is strongly dependent on the intellect, and as it is, the overwhelming dependence on the intellect is a problem that has plagued humanity for eons.

THE ATTEMPTS TO UNDERSTAND LOVE

In the attempts to understand love, the sciences analyze the body systems in the hopes of understanding certain body chemicals, nerves, and brain functions at play when one claims to be "in love." As a result, they conclude that our feeling of love is driven by certain chemicals in our various body systems, and that these chemicals are secreted and heightened during the various "love episodes" experienced by humans.

Now, what the sciences do not address, or comfortably avoid, is this question: What happens to the perceived love when all the chemicals wear-off from their effects? Does the perceived love cease to exist afterwards? The physical observations based on extensive studies might possess some validity, but what the sciences lack – the *missing link* – is the understanding of the *core* or *genesis* of how such a response came about in the first place. This is in essence asking the question: Where does it stem from? It is obvious that something had to trigger that feeling or emotion, and such a trigger happens for a specific purpose. Thus, it is apparent that science can only give a limited view on this subject because it deals largely with that which is provided in the physical world and can be quantified.

The concept of love is definitely not quantifiable, as there is no lever that can ever be concocted by the human intellect – no matter how advanced it is – that will accurately gauge or measure the totality of this phenomenon in humans. Therefore, it is improbable that they can derive sufficient answers to that which they cannot see because it emanates from the core – the physically unobservable parts – of the human being. Such matters are imponderable by the scientific mind and will remain that way. To escape the intellectual box of limitations, *we must balance the use of the intellect with the innate perceptive capabilities of the spirit.*

Now, since the sciences do nothing to answer the real questions as to the origin of love and what drives it in so many humans, as they lack the appropriate tools and knowledge base to shed light on this subject, this matter is then relegated or categorized as belonging to the religions. In which case, many seekers look to various religious sects for the answers. Unfortunately, many of those who turn to religious sects only receive grains of truth, which come in the form of *half truths.* And as if that was not bad enough, in some cases, they receive absolute lies from their many leaders.

In view of the foregoing, it must be vociferously pronounced that the original writings, teachings, and messages provided in the many scriptures from the past may not in themselves be misleading or meant to be that way. What is misleading however are the various distortions and misinterpretations perpetrated by the many persons who come across these writings and scriptures. To make matters worse, in some cases, these gross distortions and misinterpretations are consciously done to suit the selfish needs of those who preach and teach them.

In most cases, the main reason for the misinterpretations stem from their understanding of the teachings as it had been past down from generation to generation. Thus, most promulgate this message without absolute knowledge or conviction in that which they proclaim. In other cases, the misinterpretations are due to a gross lack of understanding of what is been said; in which case, individuals concoct their own version of events to suffice. This is so because of the use of parables and proverbs in an attempt to provide answers to some of the questions that were posed. However, what many fail to realize is that some of these proverbs, although seemingly vague and open for interpretation, were more applicable to their times, and more pertinently, to the specific scenario or situation which was being addressed. Also, some were allegoric and symbolic teachings not meant to be taken literally. Sadly, many wrongly apply those teachings today.

For those who do not get the answers from the workings of their intellect or the various religious factions, there is the tremendous reliance on the teachings of the secular world. As it is, secular teachings are the newest forms of organized thought because they are made up on the spot. For many, this path is the easiest to follow because it is not bugged down by scientific and religious rhetoric. With the secular movement there are no guidelines on the matters of love. The tacit code of conduct is to simply follow the "in thing to do" as of the moment as long as it "feels good" – while disregarding the consequences.

Those who follow the secular movement rely greatly on the gawking and emulation of public figures and famous persons. Some naively believe that with fame and all the material possessions at their disposal these persons must have the answers. Now, are those who make such assertions right in that line of thinking? Sadly, in most cases, the answer is No! All we need to do is to look at the lives they lead – as reported through the various media outlets. In doing so, it should become obvious that many of these famous persons are also searching for answers. As such, following in their footsteps will ultimately plunge many individuals into numerous untoward experiences, as they are bound to follow those who know not where they are going.

As a result of the many inconsistent messages provided to the masses, it is no wonder that many ascribe to the notion that love is a mystery. Now, it is important to note that those who think of love as a mystery simply do so because they look at it from the wrong viewpoint. This is similar to the actions of an individual who might try to read a book upside-down. To understand this so-called mystery, he/she must turn the book right-side up. Only then can it be seen for what it truly is. *True love in creation is as clear as night and day.*

Now, with all these misleading and incomplete answers, where can an earnest seeker turn for answers? To understand the origin of love in creation, it is important that we look at the genesis of humanity. As human beings, when we look at our birth into this world, it is apparent that in the *ideal cases*, our earthly existence is as a result of the true love shared by our parents. The love shared by parents is the *original spark* that provides the platform for a new sprit to be born into the physical sphere of existence. With the birth into this world, this new spirit is granted the ability to experience, grow, and potentially contribute positively to the world. This analogy is a very simple way of understanding the beginning of our journey on earth.

In order to fully understand love, we must look at the physical world as well as the spiritual realm of living. Only through this can humans get a complete view. In having a spiritual basis of understanding, we are bound to know the essence of true love. To do this, we must look at its *primordial origin* – the "Source."

THE ESSENCE OF LOVE

True Love is the genesis of all. The provenance of all in creation is as a result of love. The original spark of human existence is as a result of the immense love and grace of the Creator. This is simply saying that the love of our Creator is the reason why all of humanity came to be and continues to subsist.

This primordial love stems from the intent to provide human beings with the opportunity to experience in the material world, and as such, grow into mature Beings. The great yearning of the human spirit to experience and hopefully grow was the breeding ground as to why humans came into a conscious earthly existence. As a result of this great yearning, the love and grace was granted onto human beings. It could be said that such love is so immense that the human vocabulary does not possess a fitting word or phrase to accurately describe it. It is truly indefinable! It is important to understand this point because our foundation of love in nature stems from this occurrence.

In order to get a glimpse of such immense love, simply take a look at all that has been given to humans in nature – the air we breathe, the sun, water, and the list goes on and on. These elements we perceive are only a *small fraction* of all that was granted to humans. When we think of the whole – the totality of creation, such love becomes incomprehensible, as it is simply beyond human understanding. We might even be compelled to ask if we deserve such love.

In trying to understand love, many utter the phrase: *"God is Love."* Could that be true? Now, though this statement is true in part, it is much deeper than that, as the essence of the Supreme Being or Creator – acknowledged by different names due to the many different languages – cannot be grasped or defined in totality by mere words. When many utter those words, it is painfully apparent that they do so without understanding the true meaning or implications of that which they utter. What does this phrase really mean? It is encouraged that we all take a minute to consciously think about it. Now, consider this: If many believe that "God is love" and in the same breath turn around to say that "love is blind," what are they really saying? This is food for thought.

Needless to say, a conscious observer will derive a mixed and confusing message from these phrases that many persons utter so freely. On that account, it is exhorted that individuals purge themselves from the belief and constant utterance that love is blind. Such a statement seemingly implies that the purpose of human existence was blind, and as we know, that assertion is a great fallacy. We must realize that there is a great purpose for humanity. The key is to find that purpose!

True love can only exist in an illuminated state of consciousness. With consciousness comes light. As such, love can never be blind. Thus, it is advised that all persons abstain from propagating messages that continue to deceive the masses. *Only those who have not entangled themselves in the web of lies and deception can clearly see the truth.*

Furthermore, it is important to annunciate that *the natural laws and principles that guide true love, as well as other forces in creation, are constant and unchangeable.* The only thing that continues to change is how humans *choose* to interpret and express them. The natural order in creation necessitates that there are principles that guide the thoughts, words, and actions of human beings. These principles maintain a balance in nature and apply to the many facets of human living. The numerous attempts to manipulate these principles to suit selfish human needs will only serve to the detriment of those who do so and those who trail along – as evidenced by the present day "love entanglements." *No human being can ever circumvent the natural laws of creation!* As a matter of fact, we are *too small* to even contemplate or attempt to do so.

Now that some light as been shed on the origin of love in creation, how then as humans do we explain the feeling we experience called love? Certainly, there must be a way to define and shed some light to help individuals get a better understanding. But, how do we do that? Well, it is simple. We must further define love and spell out its principles.

2

DEFINITION OF LOVE

TRUE LOVE IS OF THE SPIRIT

True love is an innate feeling which stems from the core of the human being as a result of a strong spiritual connection which manifests in the physical or material world between two or more persons. Simply put, it is a connection that transcends the physical. In the material world, it is the ability granted to humans which enables us to feel a kinship and closeness to one another. Now, in giving this definition, it must be emphatically pronounced that the use of the word "spiritual" is not meant to have any religious connotations, nor is it used in a religious context. It is used to describe the non-physical and immaterial part of the human being – the spirit or spiritual core of all earthlings.

For better understanding, it is encouraged that you ask yourself this simple question: What animates me? Please take a second to think about this. Now, with thorough cogitation, it is my hope that you might come to the realization that the animation of the human being comes from the core of our Being, and not the brain, as some might believe. The brain is simply a tool for the general functionality of the human body. It also serves as a reasoning faculty. What animates the human being is much deeper than the physical. This is where the feeling of true love stems and emanates from.

This definition of love can help present a better understanding because it serves to provide a more comprehensive view. It serves to show that the love we feel for someone stems from the innermost core of our Being. It is therefore injudicious to define, justify, or explain any feelings or emotions shrouded in superficial desires as love. *True love does not exist without a spiritual foundation and connection!* It is important to know that the foundation of any union or relationship must stem from a spiritual connection and harmony between persons.

Now, for further understanding, some might wonder if love is a feeling, an emotion, or something else which is beyond the scope of basic human understanding. *Love is an innate feeling which can elicit the many human emotions.* In light of that, it is important to note that one of the greatest misunderstandings of love is the assumption that it can elicit negative emotions. That assumption is sorely unfounded! It only seems to be that way because of the misguided and inconsistent actions of humans. The original and true intention of love is to ennoble human beings. It is meant to encourage positivity; as such, should only elicit positive emotions. True love was meant to bring out the best in humanity!

Although many tend to focus intently on the romantic and intimate aspects, love is not restricted to these aspects alone. There are many dimensions of true love, such as that between children and parents, siblings, or a dear friend. It is undeniable that the strong feelings of fondness towards these persons are due to somewhat indescribable connections. I am sure that many will concur that these strong bonds and connections go way beyond the physical. In light of that, it is only commonsensical that these strong bonds emanate from the spirit of human beings – the core of all persons. As such, we must also realize that *true love can only exist between parties when the foundation of the relationship is void of ulterior motives in our thoughts, words, and deeds towards each other.*

It is obvious that there is something within humans that drives the feeling of love, and the *key* to understanding love is to thoroughly and consciously assess what drives it. This is essentially asking the question: What is the impetus for this feeling or emotion? Or another way to address this is: How and why do I feel this way? The lack of understanding on what drives love accounts for one of the reasons why many individuals have been led astray on this matter. This is so because they are misinformed about the principles that constitute true love, but more importantly, how it should be expressed. They do this by defining and expressing love in the most mundane and superficial ways imaginable. And in so doing, they are greatly misguided in understanding the purity and essence of what it was truly meant to be for humanity.

Due to this great misunderstanding, many fall into the category of the "mystified." This is so because they wrongfully assume that they can manipulate another into loving them, or better said, they presume that they can *lure* another into "falling in love" with them. In the attempt to do this successfully, they employ all deceitful tactics that the mind can conjure up. But, in doing this, what they fail to realize is that if the connection between the parties is not "spiritually validated," or "destined to be," all these tactics and ploys will continue to no avail. Subsequently, when all the attempts fail, they then speak negatively of love; which in turn leads to the general belief that love is a mystery. However, the truth remains that *love is not a mystery!*

THE "DRIVER"

What is of utmost importance in the assessment of true love is the *"Driver."* The driver speaks to the reason we feel the way we do. In essence, it is simply asking the question: What is the driving force? This is of great importance because if the driver or "push" for what many perceive to be love is derived from the calculations of the intellect or any misguided and selfish agenda, then such cannot be defined as true love.

To better understand the concept of the driver, let us take a look at an example most persons can easily relate to. Let us assess the maneuvering of a vehicle. As we all know, the driver of a vehicle is the one who controls and pushes its movement. Now, if the driver of a vehicle is uninformed about the rules of the roads, his/her judgment is likely to be impaired, thus there is a greater likelihood for an accident to occur. In using the same logic, it is clear that if the driver for what many perceive to be love is impure and stems from misinformation, they only expose themselves to the possibilities of unfavorable experiences – which easily could have been averted. If the main driver for what humans perceive to be love is solely based on the material or physical, then any union or relationship that procures on that basis is bound to lack substance, and as such, will fail at some point in time.

In most of the cases we see today, the driver for attempting to build a relationship stems solely from what many call an "attraction." Now, although an attraction of "homogenous beings" is very important in the building of a relationship or union, unfortunately, the attraction many speak of is solely of the physical. Sadly, a vast majority of the unions and relationships that exist today are as a result of such superficial attractions. We must realize that it is highly inconceivable that any relationship built on physical superficialities will grow to become substantiated or even endure the test of time.

True love can only exist absolutely devoid of any superficial desire and attraction. The driver in the purest form of true love must emanate from the spirit core of humans. Therein lies the true connection that can lead to a harmonious earthly existence for all. The best example to illustrate this is to look at the love many individuals feel for their parents, and vice versa. This could be said to be the purest of all in the physical world because it is not tainted by superficial, selfish, or material desires. That is so because it stems from the inherent part of humans driven by the spirit. In the ideal cases of human living, the feeling of love is not in any way affected by the most superficial or debased considerations such as social standing, financial status, height measurement, or physical appearance. Rather, it emanates from the spirit and is devoid of meaningless judgments.

This logic also strongly applies to marital unions in that both parties are destined for a purpose, therefore a harmonious union can only occur devoid of superficial desires or considerations. Only when the driver of love for a union is set on the right foundation can it blossom and grow aright. Anything else is a farce!

Now, some might argue that love is indeed "blind" because of the perception that when we love another we are completely blind to all factors. Well, in actuality, in the cases of true love, it is the other way around, in that individuals can clearly see and perceive all the factors with *20/20 vision*, and consciously choose to love and accept those around them. Hence the love they feel is shrouded in "light not darkness." We must see things for what they truly are. Only then does true love exist. In the matters of love, we must not blind ourselves to the realities around us. *True love is seeing people for who they are and accepting them as such.*

In the hopes of understanding love, some wish to possess an ability to read and understand the thoughts of others in an attempt to assess what another might truly feel. Now, since there is no sufficient lever or devise to accurately and unmistakably measure the true feelings of humans, how then can we determine that which is true love? Well, the answer is simple! We must openly assess our *motives* or *the spark* – the animating factor – for such a feeling of attraction to another. This is where we can find the right answer! If we are consciously aware of ourselves and our surroundings, it is inconceivable that we can be deceived by what lies solely on the surface.

Where many go wrong is in making decisions solely by what the surface presents – making decisions only by what they see or are told. It is important to explain that the superficial is that which is only on the surface. Making a decision on that basis is equivalent to attempting to write a comprehensive summary of a book simply by what is written on the cover. It is very obvious that we must read the work in its entirety before ascertaining a complete and accurate synopsis. Therefore, in the matters of love, we must not be swayed by that which can be deceitful. We must always look deeper! In doing so, it is easier to assess the true intentions of those around us. As such, the talent of mind-reading will be unnecessary because we can easily perceive what lies within the *real person*, and not the potentially deceitful physical appearances. *The answers are always apparent! It is up to each and everyone to open their receptive antennas to get the real message.*

When most speak of love, the focus for the average person anywhere in the world tends to be directed towards a physical companionship with *any* member of the opposite sex. To some, any member of the opposite sex they come across is considered "fair game" in the hopes to develop love. With that frame of mind, what they fail to realize is that *the physical can only be validated when the spirit of a human being is in charge of his/her thoughts, words, and deeds.* If not validated by the spirit, the act of seeking love from another might solely be based on misguided and selfish desires, which does absolutely nothing for the betterment and advancement of the human being as a whole.

Now, for better understanding, let us take one example that illustrates those who perceive and think of love solely on the physical or material. We can do this by looking at the actions of persons who frequent public venues "in the search for love." Some of these persons do so with the hopes of building connections – superficially and artificially – solely as a result of satisfying their so-called "uncontrollable physical needs." In most cases, this search will occur in scenarios in which these persons judge each other on meaningless and superficial physical appearances such as their pretty faces, long legs, or social status. Needless to say, they are bound to build a connection that was destined to fail from its inception. Only time will serve as proof!

What is more astounding about these activities is that some individuals do this as they are totally oblivious to the fact that a human being is a lot more than the physical. In actuality, our physical appearance is only a cloak which shrouds the true human. The true human is the spirit and that which emanates from within. Any decision made solely on physical superficialities can only lead one down the road to untoward experiences. Now, I did not say that with the intentions of disregarding the physical, because the physical cloak of a human being is meant to serve a purpose. The main purpose of the physical cloak is to serve as a covering or clothing which enables the spirit of humans to navigate the physical world. The idea of assessing a potential life partner based on this criterion without first assessing what lies within is preposterous!

The fact that true love stems from the core of human beings serves to teach us that we must be in tune with our *inner self*. That will ensure that we do not move solely by impulse or instinct. It will also ensure that there is absolute conviction and a great purpose in all we choose to enact. It is appalling to witness as many individuals become greatly engrossed in the many frivolities of living, insofar that the true purpose of their existence on earth becomes a non-issue. As such, the "pursuit of love" becomes a mode of living. As it is, some find it easier to go through life by constantly wallowing in jolly merriment while they claim to look for love. These persons must realize that such behavior only serves to drag them away from the real purpose of their existence – which every individual must consciously strive to discover and enact. The further we strive in acts and beliefs that do not align with natural laws, the more removed we are from the "truths" in creation. Consequently, this detour leads many into numerous unwarranted experiences.

Further along this line, a major source of misleading information on the subject of love comes from the many published works on the subject. They come in the form of those who spew misleading "love advice" to the masses. Most of these writings only seem to provide readers with misguided information on the various silly rules, strategies, games, tricks, and tactics on how and where to "acquire" love. Unfortunately, these misguided teachings lead many into self-destructive acts in the drive to falsely and artificially drum-up love with individuals they were probably not meant to be with in the first place. For those who seek *false love* by employing silly rules and tricks, the results of such actions will manifest in numerous unpropitious experiences – as can be observed in the lives of many today.

The employment of such silly tricks in an attempt to falsely build something that was inherently not meant to be has led to the great "trivialization of love." *Love is not a game* to be trivialized as a mundane activity. It is not to be used as an excuse to appease ourselves only as a temporary fix during a low emotional state of mind. Rather than focusing on the numerous intellectually constructed strategies and tactics, which are silly at best, it will behoove all of humanity to strive to know the principles at play in creation and consciously adhere to them. Only in doing so are individuals free from the burdens of unnecessary experiences as they continuously search for love in the wrong places, and ultimately, with the wrong persons.

THE CONSTANCY OF TRUE LOVE

True love is constant not mercurial. True love is not fickle. Though it exists in constancy, it must also grow. The show of love from day one should remain constant and grow till the end of a lifespan. Any show of affection on a temporary basis should never be misconstrued as love. Unfortunately, those who provide rules and strategies to their clients have attempted to turn something so sacred into a useless game, of which no one is a winner. In the end all parties tend to lose. We must realize that *when there is true love both parties are winners because there is equal fulfillment and ennoblement.*

Those who follow faulty teachings or advice are encouraged to focus solely on the false acts and deeds by others to prove love to them, and vice versa. For instance, during the courting phase, many women are *conditioned* to expect chivalrous deeds from men, as such a behavior is proclaimed to be a sign or determinant of love. Now, what they fail to realize is that if such deeds are done as a pretentious and temporary attempt by the male as a way to "seal the deal," then any relationship that might develop under such a situation will not pass the test of time. This is due to the fact that the show of affection is only temporary and mercurial because it is bound to change with time.

With the existence of true love, both parties will naturally and effortlessly gravitate towards each other without having to intellectually calculate their next move. No rules! No strategies! No tricks! No tactics! No games! All they do will happen naturally. It is unfortunate to watch those who fall victim to misinformation by adhering to misguided teachings that encourage the employment of tactics and games. What do they really seek? Do they seek long-lasting harmonious relationships? Or do they seek meaningless relationships which are only temporary? In adhering to the misguided teachings of others, they now expose themselves to the practice of constantly hopping from one candidate to the next in the great search for the so-called "elusive love."

Nature has taught us that whatever is wrong can only bring hurt and heartache. So how do we explain the misgivings and negative experiences suffered by individuals when they claim to love another so dearly? Well, there are two possible reasons. The first reason is that the feeling being misconstrued as love is something else driven by an unhealthy emotional response. The second reason is that these individuals do not understand the definition of true love and the principles that guide it, thus making them susceptible and vulnerable to unwarranted love entanglements. This is like driving into obstacles and congestions in an otherwise open roadway.

In the great misunderstanding of love, there are many feelings which humans tend to misappropriate as love, some of which include physical attraction, lust, affinity, and emotional dependence. If we were to take a magnifying glass and focus intently on the acts many employ when they claim to love another, we will find a preponderance of negative traits and characteristics in humans such as: wrong desires, selfishness, hatred, vanity, deceit, and superficiality.

What many now claim to be love is actually not true love. Some of the behavior and actions of those who claim to love another remains a puzzle to those who understand the principles of true love. In some cases, the actions of these persons pale in comparison to the behavior and actions that constitute true love. In genuine love, that should not be the case! It is painfully apparent that humanity has greatly deviated from the natural paths of living. If human beings lived aright such occurrences would not exist.

THE PURITY OF TRUE LOVE

True love encompasses the totality of all the positive and pure virtues within humans. It is defined by the purest of human virtues such as *trust, compassion, forgiveness, honesty, respect, support, commitment, loyalty, kindness, and altruism.* Though there are many other attributes and virtues that are present in the cases of true love, these stated ones are paramount. Without all these elements in place, it is inconceivable that any union or relationship will stand the test of time. It is painfully apparent that the reason why some believe that love is blind is as a consequence of knowing that some of these virtues or elements are absent from their unions or relationships. Thus, it is only plausible to come to the conclusion that they cannot all be possessed by one person. We must realize however that these innate virtues should not be dormant or scarce to find in the average individual. Every individual should possess all these virtues. Why they choose not to enact them remains a great puzzle!

Now, when we speak of love, there is the tendency to focus intently on the aforementioned virtues, and in so doing, we tend to forget the fact that *true love is also defined by its severity.* This notion is famously described and understood by many individuals as "tough love." The fact that love is meant to bring out the best attributes in all of humankind does not mean that we are to blind ourselves to those who consciously take us for granted. *It is unwise to continuously give unto those who have proven that they are not deserving or worthy of such.*

Sadly, as it is, some individuals remain in disharmonious unions or relationships because they believe that it is impossible to find a congruous mate who possesses all these virtues; and as a consequence, they attempt to *settle* for anyone who possesses just enough to get them by. Why should that be the case? The "settling" in these cases stems from the cries of many men and women that there are "no good" or fit partners for them in the world, so they are prepared to go for the next best thing. Well, we can see the result of such practices today!

I do not advise those who should not be in relationships to go out and seek them. However, for those who are destined to have partnerships to aid their fulfillment on earth, the key to ensuring that one is prepared for the right partner is to first *love and know yourself*. Only in loving and knowing yourself is it possible to know the right partner destined for you. It is not advised to seek partnership with another until you are fully aware of your propensities. Only in strict awareness of oneself is it possible to be able to accommodate and grow harmoniously with another.

Without a strict awareness of ourselves, it is easy to believe that love is blind because such a belief might seem to make the untoward experiences in a disharmonious relationship or union acceptable. That misguided logic has plunged many individuals into living in a false and deluded state. Many persist in such lifestyles as they are aware of the occurrences that do not constitute true love, but consciously ignore or tolerant the other whilst remaining in chaotic relationships.

Consider this: If love were truly blind, it is safe to say that divorces will not exist. This is because those who become aware that their unions are disharmonious would still remain in them under the justification that they are totally blinded by the so-called love. The evidence that the divorce rates in the world are staggering is in direct correlation with the fact that love is not blind. In most cases, many of these persons only finally opened their eyes to the faults that were apparent from the inception of the union, which they were either totally unaware of or blindly chose to ignore. We must all realize that rather than blindly jumping into the wrong unions or relationships, it is apt that we all take our time to openly assess all that can befall us. Only then have we prepared ourselves to make better life decisions. Hence we prevent the occurrences of unwarranted experiences under the claims of love.

In light of all we have touched on thus far, it is important to note that the ability to love oneself and consequently to love another must be done in a totally illuminated state. Only in a true illuminated state of being is it possible to love oneself and transpose true love to others. The knowledge that comes from understanding the truths of living is essential in helping all those who consciously strive to live aright.

The true understanding and enactment of love is bound to obviate us all from unnecessary suffering in the name of love, as those who understand the essence, constancy, and purity of love will never experience unnecessary love entrapments. To achieve this feat however, they must remove themselves from the bondage of misinformation and distortions set forth by others. All persons must in turn free themselves from unhealthy love entanglements. Therein lies the pathway to the true understanding of love!

3

THE VIRTUES

Thus far we have learned that true love encompasses the totality of all the positive and pure traits within humans, because it is defined by the purest of human virtues such as trust, compassion, forgiveness, honesty, respect, support, commitment, loyalty, and altruism. These virtues speak to the inherent goodness of all earthlings. However, in awareness of that, we must keep in mind that *love is severe*.

It is undeniable that the aspect of love that is most often overlooked or omitted by the masses at large is the fact that it is severe. Most of the time, many comfortably ascribe to the soft, weak, and overly indulgent notions of love. Unfortunately, in most cases, ascribing to such a notion does not serve them well. Therefore, in order to understand the truths of love, it is important to be cognizant of its severity.

WHY IS LOVE SEVERE?

The severity of love means that love bears consequences for any wrong actions. This remains true whether our actions are based on misinformation, misguidance, or a lack of knowledge. As it is, there are those who comfortably believe that ignorance is bliss. Well, in the matters of love, as in any other pertinent aspects of human living, it is clear that *ignorance only presents a direct pathway to suffering*. For example, let us take the case of an *innocent* child enticed by the beautiful flaring from the flames of an open fire, and through immense curiosity, the child proceeds to put his hand in the fire. Now, unfortunately for that child, his innocence or ignorance about the adverse effects of fire will not protect him from the potential burning and pain that will ensue. Now, in the case of children, the slight ignorance in action is excusable, as they just do not know better. However, for adults who engage in self-destructive activities, ignorance is no excuse!

To thoroughly assess the severity of love, it is important to pose a question which has baffled many since the beginning of our existence: "If the Creator loves us, why does He allow us to suffer?" This is a very good question because it denotes that on some level those who ask such questions are striving to understand the laws of creation; or simply, on a personal level, trying to understand why they or those around them suffer.

To answer that question, I will pose yet another question. Consider this: Does the fact that a parent disciplines a wayward child mean that the parent does not love that child? This question in itself contains the answer! It should be obvious that the act of punishing or disciplining a child is the utmost showing of true love for that child. It is a measure that ensures that the child becomes aware of his/her wrong doing and hopefully makes the necessary corrections.

The fact that we suffer is a sign that we have striven away from the natural ways we were meant to follow, and as such, we get many unpropitious experiences – which many define as suffering. The natural law operating here is a "sowing and reaping reaction." Simply, you get what you give. This is the "Law of Accountability." This law is automatic! The fact that some individuals dauntlessly turn around to question the love of the Creator is a sure sign that we as humans do not take *responsibility* for our actions. In not taking responsibility for their actions, some turn around to blame another for that which they brought upon themselves. This is similar to the act of an individual who consciously uses a sharp blade to cut himself, but stupidly turns around to blame his neighbor for the bleeding that ensues; or an individual who indulges in overeating and then turns around to blame another for the weight gained due to his intemperance. Such actions do not denote self-responsibility and accountability! If the masses do not come to a greater sense of awareness that they are *solely* responsible for their suffering, such suffering is bound to continue.

Love is justice and justice lies in love. It is important to clarify that the justice I speak about is not the idea of justice constructed by the human brain, which is largely deceitful, inconsistent, corrupt, cunning, and worst of all, discriminatory towards the underprivileged. As a matter of fact, in some circles, many have the temerity to boast of having the ability to buy justice. Thus, they are essentially buying their *earthly freedom* with the "best defense money can buy." As such, human constructed justice is largely a joke!

The natural justice in creation is indiscriminate as it stems from the infinite power of the Creator. In assessing the natural laws at play in creation, it is apparent that no one is punished unjustly. *No human being who treads aright will encounter undue suf-*

fering! With that in mind, it is painfully clear that those who suffer in unnatural *self-imposed* love entanglements have no one else to blame but themselves. *It is advised that all persons should look at themselves and assess why they suffer; only in doing so do they mitigate or obviate further suffering.*

THE VIRTUES DEFINED

As I begin to speak about the aforementioned virtues that denote true love, it is important to be aware that in order to accurately apply them in our lives, we should all have a thorough understanding of what they are. Any misunderstanding of these virtues is bound to lead the masses to wrongfully indulge others under the claims of love, as is evident in the daily occurrences around us. To fully comprehend them, it is imperative that we define them in a way that we delve deeper into what these definitions mean, as well as their applicability in our lives. Now, in assessing these virtues, we must start with trust.

Trust is the unswerving confidence in the character, strengths, abilities, and potentials of someone. Trust is an important foundation on which any union or relationship must be built upon. In view of this, some might be apt to wonder what the connection is between love and trust. Love and trust are strongly related in that without one the other cannot formulate. Without the foundation of trust, true love is non-existent. As it is, in all relationships, but most especially in the matters of marital relations, trust is of paramount importance. *True love can only blossom to its fullest potential if a union is built on the utmost level of trust in one another.*

Utmost trust in another denotes that we are aware and confident of their person. Therefore, it is easy to vouch for them without hesitation. It is impossible to trust someone if there is no confidence in their character or person. The trust in another should come as a result of a strict alignment in the way they think, speak, and act.

For individuals to coexist in consonance there must be commonality and uniformity in the way they think, speak, and act. This should happen without great inconsistencies. It is highly inconceivable that individuals who do not have great commonality in their thoughts, words, and deeds can coexist harmoniously; thus, it is unlikely that a solid foundation of trust can be built. Such a statement does not imply that for a relationship or union to flow in consonance both parties must think exactly alike. No, that is not the case! Rather, it simply means that there must be a common frame of thought and reference for there to be a solid foundation on which trust can be built and continue to grow. *With true love the trust built will serve as an unbreakable bridge that connects both souls. Trust guides everything!*

The *severity of trust* is profound because once broken it is difficult and almost impossible to gain back. This is because it is very fragile as it can easily be taken away when misused or taken for granted. Ideally, trust was meant to be an establishment in any relationship or union. However, due to the wrong ways of humans, it is now something that must be proven and attained from another. As such, in most cases, *trust must be earned.*

If a relationship or union is defined by true love no party will ever attempt to take the trust of the other for granted. It could be said that trust is a valuable commodity, and we should not act in ways that will devalue such a commodity. Rather, we must act in ways that maintains and increases its value over time. It is therefore unwise to place trust in those who are not deserving of it. Such credulity can make an individual susceptible to being taken advantage of by others. We should only trust persons who have proven by their numerous actions, thoughts, and words that they are worthy of it. This idea is important because those who are trustworthy prove that by their deeds *overtime*. It is injudicious to credulously place trust in another at impulse without thoroughly assessing their character, strengths, abilities, and potentials. To obviate ourselves from the suffering that may ensue due to misplaced trust, we must be aware of ourselves. This requires strict alertness in our everyday dealings.

Any union or relationship that is not built on trust is bound to fail. The dismemberment of many unions and relationships is most often a result of a great breach of trust – due to the fact that some take it for granted. This should come as no surprise to many because it is unimaginable that any union or relationship can survive the test of time without the true existence of trust between parties. Therefore, it is advised that we all look diligently before we place trust in another. We must not vainly claim to trust another under the misguided guise of love for them. Now, in saying that, I do not encourage that we get in the habit of automatically distrusting everyone we encounter. Such behavior will get us nowhere. What I am saying in essence is that we must be aware of those in whom we place trust. *Not everyone is trustworthy!*

Compassion can be defined as one's consciousness of sympathy or empathy for another who is in great need of help. Compassion for another does not necessarily stop at the point of being conscious and sympathetic towards their plight, it is also defined by one's intent or desire to alleviate the misfortune or problem.

The beauty about this feeling in humans is that it is not relegated or exclusive to those we love. It is easy to feel compassion for a friend or even a stranger who is in need of some help or a pick-me-up. But, it is important to note that the idea of showing compassion to another denotes that those persons are indeed worthy of such. I must make it clear that I do not encourage anyone to apathetically look over those who are truly in need and have proven by their many actions that they are worthy of help. With that said however, it is important to note that there are those who continually take the wrong paths and make wrong decisions in the hopes that another will be readily available to shower them with some compassion and clean up their mess.

The notion that love is blind has led many to become puppets of others who toy with their emotions at will. There are those who consciously misbehavior with the surety that another – who they claim to love – will always be around to bail them out from their continuous mischievous conducts. This is one case in which many become victims due to the misunderstanding of what true love and compassion was meant to be. Though it is natural to feel compassion for those in need of help, we must not allow another to continually take us for granted under the guise or claims of love. Doing so is bound to breed an unhealthy relationship for all parties involved.

The *severity of compassion* in such cases might require that we allow those who continuously engage in the wrong deeds to fully experience that which they have created for themselves. This should be done with the fervent hope that leaving them to deal with their self-imposed predicament will spark some consciousness in them, thus awakening them from their deep slumber. In essence, it is helping them help themselves. That is true love! In continuously helping persons who are unworthy, we are likely to breed shiftlessness of the body, mind, and soul. Love and compassion does not encourage indolence in another!

Forgiveness is the act of giving up or ceasing to feel resentment towards another as a result of their wrong doing. Forgiveness requires that we consciously *let go* of all negative feelings and thoughts that have the potential to emotionally weigh us down. To forgive another demands that we have reconciled whatever may have been done and have now totally absolved the situation. A major component attached to the notion of forgiveness is the ability to *forget* what had occurred. Holding resentment towards another is unhealthy for one's Being. Doing so does absolutely nothing to enrich our body and soul. To all those who have a difficult time forgiving and forgetting, I urge you to alleviate yourself from unnecessary burdens. Just simply let it go! *When there is true love we are bound to forgive without keeping notes of past deeds!*

Now, although the ability to forgive and forget is exhorted, the fact that we forgive and forget comes with the strict stipulation that we do not indulge others. We must take corrective actions when necessary to obviate further occurrences. That is true forgiveness! Continuously forgiving persons who do not take conscious attempts to mend their destructive ways is bound to breed disharmony, contempt, and in some cases, hatred. This is not the way to live!

In assessing the *severity of forgiveness*, it is important that we look at the principles many abide by. As it is, many individuals believe and follow the principle of "turning the other cheek." Now, the great flaw in the interpretation of this principle becomes all too apparent when we see those who believe they must *continually* turn the other cheek when wronged by another. The strict adherence to this principle is flawed because there is the great tendency of certain persons to take advantage of another if given the leeway. Literally and figuratively speaking, if given the opportunity, there is the possibility that these persons will continue to slap all cheeks presented to them, and will continue to do so until one has a swollen face and is facially unrecognizable. One slap on the cheek should be enough for an individual to take corrective measures!

In some cases, a dismemberment of the union or relationship will be needed to mend the situation. Such a decision might be necessary in cases in which the core foundation of trust and respect has been so greatly broken to a point of no return. In light of the fact that we must forgive the deeds of another, we must also realize that it is inconceivable that anyone can maintain harmonious relationships with those they have not wholeheartedly forgiven, as past deeds are bound to be brought up in the future. In other cases, a dismemberment of the relationship might not be necessary. However, parties must meet at a common ground; in which case, conscious steps must be taken to obviate the occurrence of such deeds in the future. Love and forgiveness does not encourage that we harbor ill-will towards another. True forgiveness denotes that we exculpate ourselves and others, thus we are free from unnecessary earthly entanglements.

Honesty is a virtue that is defined by one's sincerity, of which an individual is honorable in their words, thoughts, actions, and intentions. It is the *decision* to be upright, truthful, and straightforward in all our dealings. In light of this, we must take note that an important word in the aforementioned statement is the word "decision." This is because one's act of honesty and truthfulness is a decision that is consciously made. That is to say that an individual can either choose to practice honesty in all their dealings or they can easily choose to be dishonest. It is simply a personal choice!

When we speak of honesty, it must be emphasized that no human being is born with the predisposition to be dishonest. It is largely an acquired behavior either due to adverse living circumstances, or in some cases, merely a pathologic pleasure to avert the truth. It remains a puzzle why some persons choose the path of living a dishonest lifestyle. It must be emphatically spelt that any man or woman who acts in such ways must not be trusted.

In looking at the *severity of dishonesty,* as well as assessing the connection between love and honesty, it is important to know that *no union or relationship built on the foundation of dishonesty, lies, and deceit will exist in consonance.* The continuous acceptance of lies and dishonest conduct under the guise of love is unwise and should be stopped! *Parties who truly love themselves will feel no need to be dishonest!* Dishonest conduct is bound to break the trust in one another, and as we know, trust is a very important component on which a harmonious union must stand and grow. True love denotes that we must not consciously indulge dishonest conduct in others. Doing so only encourages them to be unapologetic to the feelings of those they hurt.

Respect is the act of holding another in high and special regard. It is a state of being in which one perceives and treats another with great esteem. Respect could also be viewed as an esteemed admiration of another. All things being right, the respect we transpose to another means that we trust them – as in the case in which a child respects his/her parents. In the assessment of respect, what is of foremost importance is the notion of *self-respect.* Self-respect is very important because the idea of truly respecting another connotes that we already respect and value ourselves. It is unimaginable that individuals who do not respect themselves would be able to transpose true respect to another. As such, we must come to the realization that respect for oneself is greatly characterized by *self-love*. *Only those who truly love themselves will respect themselves!*

The relationship between love and respect is such that without one the other cannot exist in its totality. That is to say that the totality of true love must come with a healthy respect for oneself and others. Hence, in order for individuals to be able to *grow in love*, they must respect one another. If a union or relationship is defined by true love, parties involved are bound to hold each other in high regard, and for that reason, will *never* attempt to mistreat or devalue the other. *When there is true love respect will be automatic!*

The concepts of respect and trust are greatly related in that they are both earned overtime. The act of respect is not something that should be freely granted to anyone – especially those who are unworthy. It is something that is accorded to persons who truly deserve it. It is easier to respect those we trust; likewise, it is easier to trust those we respect.

In many cultures, it is admonished that we must "respect our elders." Well, ideally, that should be the case. However, there are some cases in which the teachings of the so-called elders are in opposition to the ethical and natural truths in creation. In such cases, it would be unwise to follow their teachings without personal conviction. That is not to say that we should consciously tread in the act of disrespecting them. It simply means that we must carefully choose those whom we place value in their opinion and advice. *We should only respect those who consciously tread aright in their thoughts, words, and actions.*

A great misassumption by some occur in instances in which the words "fear" and "respect" are used synonymously. Some believe that fear of another means that we must respect them, or that we must respect those we fear. To that, it must be emphatically spelt that the needless fear of a destructive tyrant or a bully is unfounded. Such persons must not be accorded any sort of respect whatsoever. In actuality, they should be relegated to the class of those unfit to be in the midst of positive thinking earthlings. The respect for another does not mean that we fear them. Rather, it means that we value and hold them in high regard due to their worthiness.

The *severity of respect* demands that we must not respect anyone who serves as a destructive tool. Doing so wrongfully indulges their destructive behavior and is bound to lead many astray. The idea that we should respect those we love should stem from the fact that they have proven overtime through their many actions and words that they are worthy to be respected and trusted. We must not allow another to take the respect we show to them for granted in the name of love. That is not true love!

Support is the act of helping and upholding another spiritually, emotionally, mentally, physically, and materially. A relationship or union built on the foundation of true love is one characterized by the unswerving support for one another. In order for one to fully support another, there must be an established element of trust and respect. By that, I do not mean that we must only support those we trust and respect, as there are cases in which we might have to render support and help to persons we do not know. What I mean is that the totality of support for a loved one must come as a result of our confidence in their character, abilities, and potentials. The support of an individual who is unworthy might serve to further help them remain in a shiftless state. That is not advised! We must also be aware of wrongfully supporting those who make conscious decisions to engage in destructive activities. *We must not consciously support a destructive force under the mere semblance of love.* Such an act truly denotes *false love!* Thus we must love and support those who are positive and uplifting forces.

When we speak of supporting another, it is very evident that some individuals tend to focus heavily on the materialistic aspect. As a result, they forget that there are more important attributes that define one's supportiveness towards another. Such instances are apparent in cases where irresponsible and absentee parents confidently proclaim that they support their children due to the fact that they provide monetary and material aid. These persons must realize that the support of a child or a loved one must come in totality and not in fragments. The provision of material things does not denote total support!

When a union or relationship is defined by true love, parties are bound to support each other without limitations. It is true that at times we might be in need of some assistance or help, and it is during these times that the supportiveness of a loved one becomes evident. However, it is important to note that *support is not one-sided; it is a two-way street!* True love and support is characterized by a "give and take relationship." Though it is a natural feeling and impulse to want to support, assist, and help our loved ones, we must be cognizant that support must only be given to those who consciously strive to help themselves and positively contribute to the betterment of humanity. This is famously understood by the saying: *"God only helps those who help themselves."*

The *severity of support* as it relates to love is that it must not be used as a tool to encourage dependence. We must not encourage dependence under the guise of love and support for another. The support we give must enable them to stand firmly. Therefore, we must only support those who strive to support themselves. We must only support those who consciously strive for the light!

Commitment is a state of being in which one is wholeheartedly engaged and involved with another. The key word in that statement is "wholeheartedly." That is because loving another cannot be done "halfheartedly." It is either fully there or it isn't! Now, that does not mean that when we love another we must blindly indulge all they do; rather, our commitment to the union must stem from the fact that said union was built on an unshakeable foundation. Thus, there is a strong basis on which the parties can relate.

It is undeniable that one of the great quandaries in the minds of many when speaking of marital relations pertains to the concept of commitment. There is the great expectation that those we perceive as potential partners should appease us with undying commitment in the grand hopes that one is bound to eventually develop love. This is not advised! Any superficial or pretentious actions taken with the hopes of *gaining* commitment from another is bound to produce disastrous ramifications for all parties involved. In doing that, there is the high probability that with valuable time wasted – which could have been directed towards better things – the love and commitment we hope to develop or strive to attain will never formulate, as it just was not meant to be.

It is injudicious to proclaim commitment to another without first building a healthy trust and respect. The hope of committing to another without first establishing a firm foundation is bound to create a disharmonious union. Doing so is similar to trying to build a house with water-drenched sand. It is all too clear that the structure will eventually crumble. We should not commit to those who do not consciously reciprocate, as there must be mutuality in the commitment between persons. The fact that love is not blind necessitates that we look deeply before we proclaim to commit to another!

True commitment is of the soul. When parties love each other, they are also spiritually committed to one another. Those who truly love each other will remain unwaveringly strong in their ties to one another. We must realize that true commitment in a relationship or union can only formulate and continue to persist when the relationship or union is built on the foundation of true love. Hence, true love only serves to strengthen the commitment between parties.

The *severity of commitment* spells that if for any reason we take the commitment of another for granted, there is the possibility that we could lose it for a lifetime. Therefore, it is advised that we must not take the commitment of another for granted. If the commitment to another does not come naturally, such a relationship or union was simply not meant to be.

Loyalty is an unswerving allegiance or faithfulness to another. The concept of loyalty with regards to love is very much similar to the aforementioned attributes of commitment. Loyalty to someone or a cause should stem from one's total trust, respect, and belief in them. When a union is built on the foundations of a healthy trust and respect for another – which are emblematic of true love, it is easy to be loyal to them. True love and loyalty go hand in hand! As it is, many ascribe to the notion that loyalty and commitment are decisions made rather than natural impulses. Could that assertion be true? Well, that assertion is only partly true. However, to explicate further, we must make the distinction between "forced" and "unforced decisions."

Forced decisions are those we convince ourselves to make even though we are not wholeheartedly in tune with these decisions. Unforced decisions on the other hand are those that happen naturally because they flow in consonance with our convictions. In the cases of true love, loyalty and commitment to one another is unforced. Loyalty is an intrinsic aspect of true love, of which with a strong bond, the decision is firm because it comes naturally. Now, with that said, we must also keep in mind that though loyalty comes naturally, people must also make a conscious decision to maintain it.

The *severity of loyalty* necessitates that we do not remain loyal to those who have proven unworthy by taking us for granted, as there is the proclivity of certain persons to consciously take advantage of those they perceive to be weak and vulnerable. In such an instance, it is unwise to give undying loyalty to these individuals. We must only be loyal to those who strive for the betterment of humanity in their thoughts, words, and actions. Likewise, it is not advised that we proclaim undying loyalty to a cause we do not wholeheartedly believe in. If we remain loyal to a cause, union, or relationship in which we are not fully committed, we are essentially perpetrating a false existence.

Altruism is defined as the unselfish concern and devotion to the needs and welfare of another. The key word in that statement is "unselfish." That is because these are the deeds we enact without any expectation of a reward or praise. These are acts we do out of goodwill without selfish considerations. With altruism, a key note of importance is that of one's *intention*. The intentions of those who claim to help must come from a pure place. They must act without the hopes of gaining something in return. Deeds performed with selfish intentions cannot be defined as altruistic.

Though it is commendable that they were helpful, we must not mistake the fact that the true intention in their act was selfish. When a union is built on the foundation of true love, it is natural for individuals to be selflessly kind and helpful towards each other. This will be evident as they freely give and take without accounting or keeping notes of all that has been done.

However, the *severity of altruism* denotes that though it is encouraged that we are kind and helpful to those in need, we must also realize that the continuum of such deeds to individuals who take it for granted only make matters worse. Consequently, the help we render must be given to those who are truly in need. True altruism is helping those in need to help themselves!

All the virtues of humans are interconnected in that they all comingle to help form a fruitful relationship or union. A key point of note as we speak about these virtues is to understand that they must all exist in *strict mutuality and reciprocality*. A one-sided effort will never cut it!

Although there are other virtues that are inherent in humans, the totality of all the mentioned virtues should be actively apparent in our relationships. The absence of one or more of these virtues does not necessarily mean that we are not truly loved or that the union or relationship is not right. However, it is a point that each individual must address.

Since we have learned some of the important virtues and characteristics of true love, it is now necessary to consciously assess our relationships and take corrective measures as we see fit. Though it is famously said that "you must know the truth and the truth will set you free," what does it benefit an individual to know the truth without consciously applying it. The acquisition of knowledge without conscious application renders it, in essence, inane. Knowing the truth is only the first step. We must in turn take the next step to consciously apply it in our lives. We must know it and abide by it! As such, we are bound to know the meaning of true love and what it can do for humanity.

4

THE BLIND PURSUIT OF LOVE

WHY IS LOVE SO HARD TO FIND?

In the gross misunderstanding of love, many become preoccupied with the great pursuit and search for it, or better said, the search for what they perceive to be love from another. As they scurry hither and yon in the blind pursuit of love, many haplessly fall into various unnecessary experiences simply because they do not realize that what they so vehemently search for is within them. That begs the question: Why search endlessly for something that you inherently possess?

It is famously known that "we must seek in order to find." This is absolutely true. However, the search for answers can only be found if and when we know what we are searching for. Unfortunately, in the great pursuit of love, many are unsure and unaware of what they are really looking for. And as a result, they are likely to search in the wrong places, and are bound to find the wrong things.

In this pursuit of love, some men and women ask, *"Why is love so hard to find?"* Well, the answer is very simple. Love is not hard to find! It is within each and everyone. Those who ask such questions are simply looking for the wrong things in the wrong places. This great pursuit of love, although in some cases done innocently, has led many men and women into *selling their souls for affection*. It has led individuals into seeking answers from the wrong people. One of the well known venues some run to for answers are of those who proclaim themselves to be Psychics. Not surprisingly, some of these persons claim to specialize in the matters of love. What an absurdity! Now, in order to examine why so many think that love is hard or difficult to find, we must first look at the modern-day practices of those who blindly seek love. This all starts with the "commercialization of love."

THE BUSINESS OF LOVE: LOVE FOR SALE

Some who turn to these so-called "Love Psychics" do so with the purest intentions to find answers to their love questions; and interestingly, most of these psychics claim to possess great insight to the *love lives* of their clients. As it is however, in most cases, all these individuals possess is the ability to prey on the vulnerability of those who mistakenly seek love or affection in the wrong places. These false-prophets sometimes set up large network businesses where they solicit phone calls from vulnerable or curious persons, in which they sometimes blatantly lie to their clients by promising them that all will be fine in their quest for love. It is no wonder that some of these businesses become very profitable so quickly. This is because they have successfully tapped on a vulnerable spot in others.

In the push for financial gain, they are feckless to the true yearnings of their clients. This is evident as they continuously prey on those who blindly look for love. Such businesses only thrive as a result of the "continuity clause" in their business practice. As such, they must find ways to maintain and grow their clientele base. Therefore, there is the proclivity to stretch the truth or even lie so as to appease the sensibilities of their clients. In essence, they tell their clients exactly what they want to hear. Such practices should cease to exist!

Now, in saying that, I must clarify that there are a handful of persons who possess clairvoyant abilities, and I do not mean to be critical of those persons. There are those who are born with natural abilities to see and perceive that which is not solely of the physical world. And most of the true psychics possess this ability so as to help themselves, their loved ones, and in some cases, humanity at large. The gross commercialization of those who market themselves as love psychics – who are really deceivers in disguise – only breeds grounds for many false-seers who are only in pursuit of monetary gain by exploiting innocent seekers.

Further along this line, the mass pursuit of love has now led to the recent advent of a wave of internet sites and gathering clubs that boast of possessing the ability to produce magical matches by finding every member their "soul mate." As it is, the search for love has now been turned into a business or trading commodity – as we do with stocks and bonds. The proud claims of many of these popular sites is that they provide a safe platform where individuals who are searching for love can post their specifications and their needs will be met by providing a match. We now seem to be at an age in which any human vulnerability can be turned into a profit-based business venture. As such, there are individuals who proudly boast of being in the "love business."

True Love is never for sale. It is unfortunate that something as sacred as love, which is inherent in nature, has now been concocted in the human brain as a business; this is synonymous to the dealings and practices of those who *sell hope* to a congregation. A strong selling point for many of these businesses is the fact that they boast of having high success rates; as such, each member is guaranteed to find his/her one true love. Sadly, in most cases, all these sites and programs are doing is exploiting the vulnerabilities of those who blindly seek love.

The truth remains that these programs only provide a platform where individuals with similar propensities can meet. It should not be misconstrued as anything more than that. Now, some might wonder why I seem to be critical of such programs. Well, I only speak the truth as evident in the happenings around us. It is important that we are all truthful in our dealings with one another. It is not natural for individuals to prey on the weaknesses and vulnerabilities of others.

The common justification for the prevalence of such businesses is the notion that individuals are now busier than ever, and as a result, they do not have the time needed to meet a suitable partner. What we tend to forget is that many people were able to find their right partners before the advent of the internet and such businesses. In light of that, it is important to note that individuals who possess an appetency towards each other are bound to meet in the natural course of experiencing. *Love cannot be forced or arranged!*

It is understood that those who establish such businesses might do so with pure intentions, but though their intentions might be pure, they must not prey on the weaknesses of others so as to sustain a livelihood. With that said however, no judgment can be cast on these persons, as those who participate in such programs do so as consenting adults. Therefore, these participants must take account for their own actions in such dealings.

In watching the acts of the masses, it is as though many "join the crowd" in this blind pursuit of love simply because they perceive that everyone in the world is doing it, so they see such behavior as a normal part of living. Now, a key point that many fail to realize or just do not know is that *love in its truest form is a by-product of a "destined union" or relationship. Love cannot materialize without a firm spiritual connection between persons.*

Now, for clarity, how do we define a destined union? Well, a destined union is simply that which was "meant to be" and predestined before the inception of one's existence on earth. The idea of blindly seeking love from those who were not destined for us is essentially going against the grain. It is a fact that when we go against the grain, we are bound to encounter numerous untoward and unnecessary experiences. The fact that many now seem to have such experiences might confuse the masses that these untoward experiences are a normal part of human living and experiencing. Alas, that should not be the case whatsoever!

EPHERMERAL PURSUITS

Those who pursue and focus on ephemeral pleasures will never understand the essence of true love. Sadly, some individuals focus on short-lived and temporary pursuits, and as a result, are quick to "give their hearts" to undeserving persons. In doing this, all they are bound to find in the endless pursuit is a temporary feeling of affection or attention from another – most likely with ulterior motives, which tend to end just as soon as the word "hello" was uttered. This in turn creates a scenario so often seen, in which individuals hop from one partner to the next in the grand hope of making a magical match. And to make matters worse, in all the frivolous hopping, they give and waste the gifts meant for their true partner to others whom they were not meant to be with in the first place. Hence wastefully dissipating parts of themselves to the many undeserving persons they come across.

It is unfortunate to see that many of these experiences happen during the teenage and youth stages in the lives of many. This is truly sad because these are the formative periods in one's life. This is a period in which individuals should be focused on more constructive activities to help stamp their earthly identity and purpose. The meaningless meandering, which is sometimes foolishly encouraged or supported by parents, generally leads to the detriment of all parties involved. It is a fact that even adults struggle with the concept of love. So how then do we expect individuals who are still in their formative years to blindly explore?

As we have come to see, in this *age of experimentation*, many naive individuals get involved in acts that were meant for a husband and wife in a committed union as a physical expression of their love. With that in mind, it is important to note that *true love can only be experienced by mature persons, because only then can the physical expression of such love be meaningful.*

Now, such a statement does not connote that youngsters do not have the capacity to love, as they can truly love their parents, family members, and friends. What I mean is that for two persons in a committed union to be able to express *all the components of love* – especially the physical, they must possess a certain level of maturity. As such, they will not jump blindly in meaningless experimentations under the guise of seeking love. Needless to say, the mass increase in teenage birth rates and unplanned pregnancies around the world is evidence of those who jump blindly in meaningless experimentations. Although there is a paucity of cases in which two youngsters might be destined to meet and start their journey together before adult age, those cases are rare and far in between. This is so because the ability to truly understand what love entails takes a certain level of personal maturity. Acts done under the pretense of love are gravely superficial and meaningless!

It is important for teenagers and youngster to experience, as experiencing is an integral part of living, however it is also imperative to teach them to tread only in positive acts. They should only be exposed to things that are appropriate for them. Since the teenage and youth ages are the formative years, it is important to ensure that the right foundations are set to help these individuals become productive participants of the world. Unfortunately, some youngsters adopt the wrong teachings of love from the romanticized messages promulgated through the numerous popular love songs and movies. And as a result, they are propelled into self-destructive behavior under the guise of love. Ideally, the true exemplification of love should come from their parents. However, sadly, in some instances, that is not the case.

Since most tend to perceive love as a complicated feeling and believe that they are entitled to *find love* at all cost, they turn to many relationship books in the quest for knowledge. It is interesting to see that many of these books produce a set of rules on how to attain the right partner. Pathetically, most of them only focus on the superficial ways of attracting, or for a better word, "hunting" a partner. As it is, they preach and teach so-called "proven methods" to *temporarily* attain the attention of another. Thus, they provide readers with lists on how to act, smile, flirt, and the best places to shop in the attempts to attract a potential mate. These writings provide percepts that men and women should abide by in the search for love; and most of these teachings come with the claims that all will be right if one simply follows "the rules." Unfortunately, these precepts and rules only turn free-thinking humans into robots. In following the misguided teachings of others, some individuals seem to move without logic or conviction in what they do, but do so anyway simply because a so-called expert says so.

Furthermore, to compound matters, these percepts are designed as a *one-size-fits-all* plan. These rules or plans are promulgated under the premise that one can build love with whomever they choose. Now, with that fallacy in mind, some individuals believe that if they act or look a certain way, they are automatically predisposed to find love. It is important to note that *when true love exists there are no precepts or rules on how to act*. Such rules only turn something that was meant to happen naturally into a game. And as we all know, a game is an activity that can yield a 50/50 chance either way. Therefore, if individuals venture into "love seeking" as an experimental game, there is the likelihood that they might come out with unfavorable results.

What some of these books tend to do is to play on the vulnerability of those who innocently look for answers. In doing this, they forget that we are all too unique to adhere to the same strategy and expect the same result. As such, it is easy to understand why so many people have a myopic view of love. Some of these popular books seem to paint a negative and gloomy picture of love. They seem to all follow a very familiar pattern, as they send out messages that portray the pursuit of love as a tough and hurtful road to travel. They also portray the journey to love as one filled with heartbreak and hardship. However, what they fail to realize or just do not know is that *the blind and misguided pursuit of love is the sole reason for the journey filled with heartbreak and hardship.*

THE JOURNEY TO LOVE: AN EASY OR HARD ONE?

As it is, there is the general belief that only in experiencing obstacles and heartache do we see the light. Now, that then begs the question: Are we meant to encounter obstacles, hardships, and heartaches in order to experience true love? The answer is an emphatic No! If humans lived aright, we were not meant to experience many of the obstacles most encounter. Rather, we would consciously and knowingly seek those who are in great alignment with us; which in turn eliminates a great number of meaningless courtships and baseless relationships.

Now, it is true that in experiencing we are all bound to make some mistakes or misjudgments, however, the importance of the mistakes we make is that we learn from them and hopefully tread carefully thereafter. In watching the actions of some, one is bound to wonder how they can justify their numerous unwarranted experiences in the name of that which they define and trivialize as love. What some individuals now seem to do is to turn the pursuit of love into an endless game of *trial and error*, in which they dabble aimlessly in the attempts to build something out of thin air. Knowing oneself denotes that we do not journey blindly with the hopes of striking gold. We must be fully aware of ourselves! Hence, we are fully equipped to understand the qualities that must be possessed by those who are prepared on our paths for a harmonious union. Dabbling aimlessly indicates that individuals are still in search of an identity, and therefore wallow with the hopes that another will determine that for them. It is important that we do not blindly venture into any scenario. We must make sure that all our experiences are taken with complete consciousness and awareness.

The knowledge of our destination means that we do not have to be detoured by "self-constructed obstacles." This knowledge and awareness spells that each individual will take a straight and unobstructed route in getting to the final destination. A perfect example of this is what we see in child prodigies. In possessing strong talents and abilities, they make it easy for their parents to nurture these talents by employing all necessary resources to help them blossom. Many of these children are brought up knowing their destination and do not get distracted from that ultimate goal.

As it is, the pursuit of love and the search for one's right partner seem to be two different goals in the minds of many. What many do not understand is that this is actually meant to be one goal. *Only in finding one's right partner will one experience true love.* So, rather than blindly looking for that which is unattainable, it is important to be cognizant of what we are really searching for. The journey to love is meant to be an easy road to travel; we must not make it a hard one.

WHAT IS THE PURPOSE OF THIS LOVE I SEEK?

Individuals who search for love should ask themselves this important question: *"What is the purpose of this love I seek?"* In thoroughly and truthfully answering this question, they are bound to realize the drive or impulse in the desire to find love. It is very clear that the search for the wrong reasons will only breed wrong results. The intention is a very important element in human living. It is the driving force for all the actions we take. Now, if for any reason our intentions are not in alignment with natural laws, we are bound to go through many obstacles and hardships – which humans often define as suffering.

The true purpose of love is to ennoble humans. Seeking love for any other reason will produce grave results! In assessing a potential union, we must take note that *if the intention of one party is impure then the foundation of such a relationship or union is wrong.* When the time comes for one to find the right partner, it is very important that both parties must possess the purest of intentions during courtship. Then and only then is it possible to truly build a harmonious union on the right basis. In light of this, some might wonder if it is possible to grow or develop love from an ill-intentioned foundation. Well, needless to say, the answer to such a query is a resounding No! A relationship that begins with ill-intentions can only persist for a while – as long as the going seems good. With such relationships, the faults are bound to show as time passes, and the partnership will eventually crumble.

The misunderstanding of love has led many to proclaim that the love they seek from another should come from one who will "complete" them. On that account, we must come to the realization *that no human has the power or potential to complete another. The truest of unions and relationships are those that are complementary.* It is important to make clear that the word "complete" is used in reference to the assumption that we as individuals are lacking something and will only be "whole" when another dictates that by coming into our lives. That should not be the case! We are who we are for a purpose; and as such we are complete. The right partner will not act as a supplementary force, but as one who complements what we bring to the table; thus creating a "balance" rather than a completion.

LOVE FADS: THE INFLUENCE OF THE WORLD

In the mass pursuit of love, many are greatly influenced by the latest *love fad* – that which is deemed socially acceptable as of the moment. The acceptability or "coolness" of such actions is heavily driven by the majority – who themselves do not know better. If the search for love is something that is influenced by the latest fad, then it only serves as a function that is temporary and will pass with time. All this tends to breed is a situation in which all followers are taken into the deep depths of immorality under the guise that they are in love with another. Unfortunately, all they are experiencing is truly "false love" – defined by meaningless and insubstantial actions.

The principles that guide true love remain constant in creation and should never be condensed to fit the latest "in thing" to do. When we look at the immense effect of popular culture on how many live today, we can cite many cases in which naive individuals have been led astray in the deluded belief that their actions fit into the norm of the day, so they must be right. Sadly, in that line of thinking, they only hurt themselves.

It is advised that we must all take a back seat and thoroughly assess the decisions we make. There is no valid excuse for ignorance! We all have to account for our actions. Therefore, it is imperative that all persons move in *full* conviction in all they do. We must not act solely by the accepted norms of the majority. It is a credo of living in most societies that "the majority rules," but if the rationale in the acts of the majority strive in opposition to the natural flow of creation, then we must stand up and correct it.

A major practice in the new love fad of the world is the lowering of one's bridge and succumbing to mediocrity in an attempt to find love. Unfortunately, this practice takes many to the land of unpropitious experiences. In finding one's true partner, we should never succumb to mediocrity in the hopes of accommodating another. The fact that an individual has to blindly tolerate another under the guise of love usually indicates that the union or relationship was not meant to be. It is important that one does not employ another as a medium or "filler" in the journey of self-discovery. I am sure that we have all heard or seen the many cases in which some individuals let themselves go in the shadows of others, and were consequently dragged into the abyss of nothingness. *True love denotes that we should never allow another to dictate our path. Each individual must take full control of his destiny.* Then and only then are we in position to find the right partner for a harmonious union.

Two major elements in the search for love are *self-worth* and *self-awareness*. These are two important driving forces in finding one's true partner. An individual who does not have a firm awareness of self is bound to search for like, and this leads to a scenario in which two blind individuals are driving a car. Needles to say, we all know how that journey is going to end. In order for individuals to be in the right partnership, they must be fully aware of themselves.

A dangerous result of low self-worth is what many refer to as the "lowering of one's standard." This seems to come into play when individuals feel as though they cannot meet a suitable partner, as they perceive their expectations or standards of a potential partner to be practically unattainable. As a result, they are wrongfully advised by friends and well-wishers that the only alternative is to lower their expectations or standards. *No one must lower their standard to accommodate another!* Doing so is the surest evidence that such a relationship or union was not meant to be. In some cases, in the tireless attempt to accommodate an inherently unfit partner, many employ a strategy of trying to "train" the other party – as one might do to an undomesticated pet. It is unwise to get into the habit of trying to train another human being. The fact that such a thought even exists is an obvious sign that this individual was not meant for you. If the differences between both parties are so great, it is inconceivable that such a relationship can pass the test of time.

In the attempts to find love, we must not delude ourselves to the apparent negative propensities of another. We must be consciously aware of that which assails us, only then can the right decisions be made. In the hopes of finding love, many become blindly oblivious to the apparent signs of incompatibility by attempting to build something only by focusing on the positive attributes. Though it is admirable that we focus on the positive attributes of another, we must be aware that the dismemberment of a relationship *always* comes as a result of the negative propensities which we chose to ignore or put aside.

When many lower their standards, they lay the grounds to meet with those who are of a different standing than persons they were meant to be with. When we compromise on our principles, we are only inviting those whom we were not meant to partner with. This can only mark the grounds for a wrong foundation, thus a disharmonious relationship.

The lowering of one's expectations or standards could also be detrimental because it breeds grounds for a matching of "negative homogenous attractions." The matching of negative homogenous attractions arises when two or more individuals meet solely on the basis of their similar negative appetencies. In that case, the basis of the partnership will be based on negative attractions. For example, let us look at the case in which two persons attempt to build a relationship based on their appetency to over-indulge in the many frivolities of human living. That is not the basis on which they should attempt to build a relationship; as one party is likely to grow out of such practices, consequently leaving the other behind. As a result, they have what is commonly re-ferred to as "irreconcilable differences." All that simply means is that the foundation was not right, as such, they were bound to strive apart.

We must not condone that which is wrong in another. That is a sure sign of incompatibility! Both parties must be equally matched in all key facets of human living in order to shape the right union. If both parties are equally matched, any differences between them will be minimal and will serve as a small area for growth. When one or both parties lower their standards to ac-commodate the other, there tends to be a *great gap* which cannot be filled. In most cases, this gap will become more apparent as the partnership progresses.

As it is, many who follow the new love fads become overly preoccupied with what members of the opposite sex are looking for. Sadly, this information is generally fed to them by the numerous magazine articles they read. In focusing on what another wants, it is as though they are prepared to mold or morph themselves to appeal to the other person's expectations. The more appropriate question should be: What are my expectations of a potential partner? Now, the purpose of this question is not to totally disregard the needs of a potential partner, as *there has to be mutual affinity for a relationship to develop*. The idea behind this question is to ensure that we are first aware of ourselves. With self-awareness we are more aware of a partner who is a great fit. Though we might be firm in our expectations of another, it is also important to assess if there is a compatible fit based on the other party's expectations as well. It is true that when we love someone we are bound to make some concessions. However, this should only be within certain confines. *We must not totally lose our identity in the hopes of building love with another.* It is unfortunate to see those who lose themselves and their identity in the search for love. That is not true love!

In addition, there are many popular media products that target the masses, and many of these very popular television shows seem to propagate a message that advocates a promiscuous lifestyle under the guise of searching for "Mr. Right" or "Mrs. Right." Some of these popular shows chronicle the lives of certain persons and their "struggles" as they hop from one individual to another in the pursuit of love and relationships. In this constant hopping, they engage in numerous immoral acts with a multitude of persons, and sometimes the engagements in these acts begin at the mere uttering of a greeting at first sight. Unfortunately, with such actions, most are conditioned to believe that another is bound to love them. This is in essence *selling their bodies for love*. In doing so, *they are only temporarily free of the body but dead of the spirit.*

Most of these programs tend to target females, as they are promoted under the premise that women now possess a so-called "newfound empowerment." Thus they should be able to experience promiscuity – as their fellow male counterparts had done for ages. Some speak with misguided confidence that the time is now appropriate for the balancing of the scales, in that females now possess the power to misbehave as males have for generations. It is almost as though they intend to fight fire with fire! And sadly, all this is done under the guise of seeking love. What a shame!

It must be said that such actions will only lead these individuals into deeper depths. Logic and common sense has thought us all *that two stupid actions can never produce a sane conclusion.* The fact that *some* males have chosen to act as wayward Beings without logic in reasoning should not mean that *weak-minded females* can justify their debased actions by joining the "club of misguided infidels." When did it become acceptable to be a proud promiscuous Being under the guise of freedom, liberation, and modernity? Consider this: If all women stand aright, who will the promiscuous and frivolous men dabble with? This is food for thought!

To a conscious observer, it is very clear that these individuals who so confidently flaunt their newfound empowerment are truly *confused*. It is very easy to see that only in a state of confusion will anyone give their precious and private gifts meant for their one true partner to a multitude of undeserving persons. There is absolutely nothing empowering in *leasing* your body to persons who view you simply as a valueless and dispensable entity. It is my fervent hope that these persons will come to understand the true meaning of self-empowerment in creation.

True empowerment is the consciousness and knowledge of oneself, which strengthens one's resolve in positive actions that only serve to uplift. Those who are truly empowered do not follow teachings that will drag them to the trenches of gross turpitude. They will not lower their bridges to the depths of self-destruction under the misguided rationale that they are empowered. A truly empowered woman or lady is one who knows herself and understands her purpose in creation. She is one who knows her worth; as such she is free and liberated. She will not feel the need to be swayed by the useless messages in popular culture promulgated by misguided persons. When a true lady stands, all men and children will take notice and fall in line. A woman who stands aright is truly a blessing, for she is bound to live in ways that will ennoble all around her.

TRUE LOVE IS NOURISHMENT TO THE SOUL

If we choose to only pursue the material or physical, we are bound to continue suffering. In the endless pursuit of love, many focus greatly on the fulfillment of their so-called physical needs. And under the guise of love, they seek persons who will provide them with physical gratification. Though it is true that the act of love-making is a natural course in human existence, we must realize that the real essence of such an act will only be truly fulfilling if both parties are destined to be, and not jokesters who seek meaningless thrills in the pleasures of the flesh. In chasing these pleasures, it should come as no surprise that many of these individuals are left with a deep feeling of emptiness after all the frivolous activities continue with nothing of substance to hold on to at the end of the day.

When a union is built on the foundation of true love, the physical act between a man and woman will serve as nourishment for the body as well as the soul and the whole Being. We are more likely and prepared to experience true love when we seek that which nourishes the soul first. Only then will everything else fall in place. Only individuals who strictly adhere to the natural laws of creations are accorded the opportunity to experience true love.

Consider this: Imagine walking through a dark room where one could easily switch on the light but consciously decides to go in with the intentions of being adventurous. Needless to say, this individual is bound to bump into many obstacles in this room. It would be more reasonable to turn on the light and walk with confidence. *If we look blindly, we will never find that which nourishes the soul.* We must not jump blindly in the pursuit of love. We must all "turn on our lights!" *We must first find ourselves before we seek love from another.* We must not aimlessly pursue love outwardly; rather, we must all look inwardly. Therein lies all the answers!

5

LOVE THYSELF

With the immense focus on the romanticized aspects of love, many tend to overlook one of the most important principles of love. That principle is to *fully and wholeheartedly love oneself*. This spells the *"Oneness of love,"* or *"Self-love."* There are many dimensions of love in creation, of which the love and respect of the Creator is of paramount importance. However, when we look at our experiencing in the material world, the love of oneself is very important. *It is virtually impossible to effectively love another if you don't love yourself*. Therefore, we must all start with ourselves!

It is an unmistakable fact that when the subject of love is at hand, most people tend to focus on the other person or persons rather than looking within themselves first. This makes it possible to understand the misgivings of those who claim to love another but do not love themselves. A vital question to ask oneself is: "If I do not love myself, how do I know how to love another and how do I expect another to truly love me?"

Now, in order to shed clarity on this matter, we must thoroughly assess the concept of self-love. What do the words "Love thyself" truly mean? Is it just another one of the meaningless phrases we use whenever we see individuals who appear to be self-destructive? Or is it used in a "counseling mode" to address acts we notice in others? The point I am trying to make in asking these questions is that we rarely utilize these words when speaking about ourselves. The focus of utterance always seems to be directed at others. On the surface, this seems like a simple phrase which needs no further explanations or analysis. However, this seemingly simple adage is extremely profound, as it is bound to shape the path individuals tread in their earthly experiencing.

The idea of loving oneself is the foundation and basis on which we act and react to those around us. But more importantly, it defines how we perceive ourselves in creation. The foundation of one's identity and purpose as a human being is greatly determined by that individual's understanding of not only the meaning but also the principles that constitute love of self. That is to say that an individual who is misguided or misinformed on the concept of love will not only misapply it to himself but will extend this misapplication to family members, friends, and neighbors.

WHO AM I IN CREATION?

On the road to truly loving yourself, you must ask yourself this pertinent question: "Who am I in creation?" Now, if the answer to this question contains numerous earthly labels, tittles, or awards, then you might be disillusioned about your true identity or purpose in creation. And unfortunately, this is bound to take you away from truly loving yourself.

Love of self demands that you do not define yourself by earthly material valuations. Societal designations and classifications are human-made constructs, and as such, are essentially meaningless in the greater scheme of things. If we bind ourselves to them, we are essentially *slaves to that which we have created*. We were born without these labels and titles, and it is a surety that we shall pass on from the material world without them. So why hold on to titles and labels that do nothing to ennoble the spirit?

If love of self is determined by meritorious labels attached by others, then one must be ready for the potential precipitous fall which might ensue. As we have seen in countless cases, the same persons who hail you will be the same persons to eventually scrutinize and bring you down. Therefore, true love of oneself should transcend all that we perceive in the material or physical world. It should not be defined by outward appearances. It must come from within. The true definition and value of humankind comes from the spirit. *Love of self is truly of the spirit.* The spirit is who you are in creation!

SELF-AWARENESS

A major part of loving oneself is to develop a strong sense of *self-awareness* as a living Being. This self-awareness means that individuals must unswervingly stand firmly and consciously tread the path that they were destined to follow. *An awareness of self is the pathway to self-discovery.*

A strong sense of self-awareness denotes that we take conscious actions that are strictly in accordance with the natural laws of creation. We must not allow another to trample on us. It is unwise to give another the license to play an unwarranted role in steering us away from that which we were destined to enact for the betterment of humanity. It is therefore imperative that we stand firm. Unfortunately, there are those who allow others to dictate their lives, and in so doing, they lose sight of themselves and their true identity. That must stop!

At this juncture, it is important to note that parents or guardians are meant to play a pivotal role in helping bestir a child into building a strong and firm *sense of identity* and self-awareness. This is very important because one's self-identity begins at the primordial stages of existence. The foundation of self starts from the earliest relationships we know – that of a child and parents. It is therefore necessary to ensure that all children are nurtured to truly love themselves. They must be aware that their identity in creation *must not* be determined by another, but must come from within. Those who accomplish great feats for humanity are individuals who are truly themselves. These persons do not limit themselves by staying within the blockades of societal norms. With conscious awareness of themselves, they allowed their inherent gifts and talents to blossom forth.

LOVE THY NEIGHBOR AS THYSELF

What happens if individuals do not love themselves? Well, that tends to lead to a scenario of dysfunctional and destructive activities enacted under the pretence or assumption of love. That is simply saying that we tend to treat others the way we like to be treated, which is most famously illustrated by the adage *"love thy neighbor as thyself."*

When we say, "love thy neighbor as thyself," what are we really saying? Often, when many utter these words, it is usually done under the assumption that we indeed love ourselves. But, what if an individual just does not love himself? To this individual, the saying might as well be: Hate thy neighbor as I hate myself. If individuals are displeased with themselves, it becomes apparent that they will transpose such to others. What this spells in plain terms is that individuals who do not effectively love themselves have the potential to become destructive forces, not only to themselves, but to those around them as well. As such, we should not be surprised when we hear the cases of those who are destructive to their neighbors and society as a whole. It just might be that they do not love their neighbor, but more apropos, that they do not love themselves.

Along this line, one of the most apparent instances of the misapplication of love are the many cases in which individuals inflict physical or emotional harm to themselves simply because another claims not to love them. Sadly, in some cases, such deplorable acts are done to *prove* their so-called love to another. Now, there is no question that these individuals might have some affinity towards the other person, however the "mode of expression" is in direct opposition to the principles of self-love. *For no reason whatsoever should anyone consciously or unconsciously harm themselves or others under the guise of love.* The act of hurting oneself under the misguided shroud of love illustrates a deep and severe level of *self-hatred*. We must not get in the habit of encouraging or wrongfully defining self-destructive actions as those that illustrate love for another. That is false love!

True love of oneself comes with the utmost level of self-preservation. This self-preservation stems from the fact that those who truly love themselves understand that their *physical body* is one of the greatest gifts granted onto them; and as such they consciously nourish and preserve themselves. True love from another should only serve to further such self-preservation. Anything in opposition of that must not be misconstrued as love! This goes in line with the belief of many that "our bodies are the temple of our Creator." Although the totality of this statement is greatly inaccurate and misleading, as human beings are *too small* in creation to even utter such words, it does present some grains of truth. It spells that as a very small part of creation, we must take care of that which has been granted to us to aid our earthly experiencing and spiritual maturity.

It is unimaginable that those who truly love themselves will partake in self-destructive acts in an attempt to gain the love and affection of another. If there is true love, no party would have to take negative actions to prove their love to another. Ideally, we do not have to prove our love to anyone, because our altruistic deeds to one another should in fact be enough evidence that the relationship is built on the foundation of true love. *True love can only serve to uplift.* Therefore, we must assess our various relationships, and if we find ourselves in conditions that are not conducive to the ennoblement and enrichment of the body and spirit, we must make decisions to rectify the situation.

SELF-WORTH

It is very important to note that a major part of loving oneself is in understanding one's worth. We must develop a *consciousness of self-worth.* Knowing your worth means that you understand your inherent value as a human being. *Loving yourself is to understand your purpose in creation and in turn to hold yourself as well as those around you to a high standard.* Now, some might wonder what I mean by "high standard." The high standard I speak of has nothing to do with the societal definition. I speak of a standard of living that is conducive to fostering one's purpose in creation. We must not allow ourselves nor should we give another the license to detour us from our goals. Without self-worth an individual is practically lost. Those without self-worth are likely to have no sense of direction, for in order to move, they must know their purpose in creation. As it is, those who lack self-worth tend to seek love from others in an attempt to validate their existence.

In a relationship or union in which one party depends solely on another to determine or validate their self worth, it is practically impossible for true love to flourish. That is because such a relationship is defined by the weaknesses of the parties. In such cases, the best case scenario would be that these individuals were just meant to be friends; in which case, they were simply only meant to help each other. Sadly, when some individuals linger in low self-worth, the automatic response is to seek out a relationship with another individual in an attempt to prop-up and rectify this deficiency. What is most appalling is that all this is done under the pretence of love.

These actions only lead to the many occurrences we see today, in which many remain in disharmonious unions and relationships under the shroud of love. And in an attempt to explicate their persistence in these parasitic relationships that stem from low self-worth, some utilize this commonly used phrase which we hear too often: "But I love her/him." As it is, these words are uttered in a lackluster effort to justify that which they know is wrong. Love is so sacred and should not be trivialized in such circumstances. The best way to describe such a relationship is that it was built on the basis of "matching negative propensities."

In order to build a union defined and built on the basis of true love, both parties must have an established self-worth. They must first figure out themselves before they seek love from another. The search for love as an aid to figure out ourselves could be a perilous road to travel. The notion of an established self-worth by both parties denotes that these individuals have worked on fully discovering themselves; therefore such a relationship can only serve to continually uplift them. The love experienced in that case will be a by-product of that which is established and was destined to be.

LOVE DOES NOT HURT!

In the great misunderstanding of love, one of the greatest fallacies believed by humans is the notion that "love hurts," or that in the experiencing of love one is bound to be hurt. The peril of harboring such beliefs is that some individuals are likely to hurt themselves if they believe that love hurts. Even worse, they are bound to encourage and indulge others who hurt and mistreat them. We must ask ourselves: Why should such a wonderful gift to humanity serve to hurt?

This negative belief of love is the groundwork for those who allow themselves to blindly accept mistreatment from others under the guise of so-called love or affection. The natural ability of humans to feel pain or hurt is a wonderful attribute given to humans. It serves as a sign that indicates disharmony in the body.

And as we all know, if we continue to ignore these signs, there could be potential harm or even death.

All things being right, pain or hurt was not supposed to be a normal occurrence of human living. It is not something that we must accept without questioning why it is happening. Painful or hurtful occurrences in our lives are great signs that there is an immediate need for corrective actions. As it is, there are those who wallow endlessly in disharmonious unions and relationships simply because they believe that hurtful behavior comes with the "love package." How unfortunate! Unbeknownst to them, these negative or hurtful feelings in their relationships are signs of a "cancer" that needs to be cured. Only in cancerous relationships will one experience hurt and pain.

True love does not hurt. True love is hurt-free and painless. The general belief and acceptance of the ridiculous notion that love hurts only justifies or breeds grounds for many individuals to accept mediocrity in their various relationships. Many of the dysfunctional relationships that are being justified under the premise that love hurts should be immediately and promptly reassessed, and if necessary, eradicated.

Now, this leads us to examine a common complaint that many grapple with unsuccessfully, in which case, they turn to friends and family members to find the answers. This quagmire comes in the form of a question: "If he/she truly loves me, why do they treat me like dirt?" Well, the answer to this question is twofold. The first answer is that the person asking the question allows this to happen. As we know, an individual will only treat you the way you allow them to treat you. Therefore you must hold yourself to a high standard, for in doing so there will be an appetency of like. The second answer is that these individuals who hurt another do not really love that person. The idea of consciously inflicting hurt on another party is an obvious sign of a lack of love. The expression of true love is exhibiting a healthy respect for oneself as well as others. This respect will never lead one to even harbor the slightest thought of hurting another. Love of oneself requires that individuals are very careful and aware of the potential consequences of their actions on those around them. If there is a healthy respect for the other party, any decisions or actions that might have adverse and negative effects will be greatly mitigated.

THE PRINCIPLES OF SELF-LOVE

On the road to effectively loving oneself, there are certain principles that we must all be aware of. These principles can help all persons tread the path that can lead to a fruitful and worthwhile earthly existence. They are meant to aid in guiding us in living in accordance with the natural flow of creation, and not in opposition. An individual who understands and adheres to these principles is the epitome of one who truly loves himself, but more importantly, understands the concept of self-love.

Love of self demands that you are conscious of yourself. Self-consciousness is very important because it spells that you are aware of all you think, say, and do. Those who truly love themselves think, speak, and act in strict alignment. They will act without inconsistencies. Love of self demands that you uphold your principles and values at all times. You must not swing in the pendulum of indecision when it comes to your values, morals, and principles. You must be firm and decisive. You must act with strict conviction in all you do!

Love of self demands that you treat your body with utmost respect. A healthy spirit resides in a healthy body. Your body is a gift which enables the spirit to navigate the material world. As such, you must nourish your body properly so as to fulfill your goal on earth. Sadly, there are those who have prematurely cut their earthly existence due to the fact that they did not respect their bodies, as they abused their bodies to a point of no return. Remember this: Your body is like a car that your spirit drives through life's journey; in order to complete this journey safely, you must maintain a car that is properly tuned and well-oiled. *Respect your body so as to enable your spirit to unfold to its fullest capacity!*

Love of self demands that you know your boundaries and limitations in all facets of living. The knowledge of our boundaries and limitations could serve to obviate us from unwarranted experiences. For better understanding, let us look at the case of an individual who indulges in excessive drinking to a point of becoming a stupor. The inability to thoroughly assess his limitations will make this person a potential nuisance to those around him. Though we are accorded the right to enjoy the pleasures of drinking in limited amounts, we must not excessively indulge. Doing so will lead one down the path to self-destructive behavior. However, with that in mind, it is important to note that it is practically impossible for individuals who truly love themselves to engage in any self-destructive acts.

Though there are many more examples which can be cited to illustrate this, the point is not to mention every scenario possible, but to open the eyes of many to the fact that we unknowingly hurt ourselves when we do not know our limitations. And as a consequence of not knowing our boundaries, we transition into the realm of self-abuse. The idea of self-love goes in strict alignment with the concepts of checks and balances in nature. That is to say that all we do must be in moderation. The indiscretion and tactless excesses in human living is one of the reasons why some suffer today.

Love of self demands that you are content with who you are and what you have been given. Never try to be like another. Let your true self blossom forth. Never let go of yourself. Those who are not content with the gifts they possess will not realize their full potentials. Such discontent is evident in the actions of those who try to change themselves to be like another. In so doing, they squelch their true abilities and talents. For no reason whatsoever should anyone attempt to be like another. Love who you are and you shall become what you were meant to be!

You must enact the unique abilities that you inherently possess. All conscious Beings must be original in their thoughts, words, and deeds. Copying the ideas of others without the conscious steps to develop and enact your own originality greatly diminishes your worth and value to humanity. This is painfully evident in the retrogression of some cultures around the world. In some of these cultures, there is the overwhelming dependence on the ingenuity, innovation, and inventions of others, thereby putting them at the mercy of those who possess the so-called "world power." I define this state of being as the "copycat mentality." In this state, many are permissive to political, social, and worst of all, intellectual hegemony by those they perceive to be governors of the earth; as such, they sell themselves short. We must come to the realization that we all have a purpose in existence; otherwise we would not be here. Therefore, it is exhorted that we all search for our purpose and take conscious steps to enact them for the betterment of humanity.

Love of self demands that you are self-assured and secure. Never compare yourself to another! No two persons are created to be exactly alike. We are all special in that we possess unique traits and abilities that are to enable us to navigate this world. Therefore, each person's path in life is different. The path taken by another is solely theirs. Another person's path must not be used as a gauge to assess your life. Granted, there are natural developmental stages of growth, but even within these, all persons are unique and must be respected for who they are.

Relativity in self-assessment is the root of insecurity. We must not judge our successes or failures by standards set by mere humans. The only standard by which we must live is that of the Creator. Judging yourself by standards set by another often leads to discontentment, which is likely to push one into trying to act, speak, or even think like another. And in so doing, you are essentially squelching your whole Being. When you suppress your true self, you create a detour from the path originally destined for your fulfillment.

The gross discontentment with oneself can be seen in the actions of those who focus attentively on the outward forms or appearances that are put forth by others. And based on these outward appearances, some go to great lengths to morph themselves into trying to be like another. These actions are more prevalent in the modern-day "celebrity worshipping." Now, I must say that there is absolutely nothing wrong in admiring those that stand aright. However, such admiration should propel you to enact your own destiny – in your way, and not in the way of another. In the history of humankind as we know it, if everyone had tried to conform into being like another, most of the inventions we enjoy today may not have come into existence. There are those who stood out because they were meant to enact something special for humanity – as we all are. You must be yourself!

Love of self demands that you do not steal, cheat, or lie to ingratiate yourself. There are those who engage in gross mendacious activities under the covering of social legality, and though they know that their actions are *ethically wrong* and deceitful, they persist in such behavior so as to ingratiate themselves in their various social gatherings. This behavior does more to devalue the social criminal than those they *legally steal* from. The devaluation of another to prop-up oneself signifies a grave sadistic disorder that needs to be addressed. For no reason whatsoever is any man or woman justified in stealing, cheating, or lying. When we steal from another we are essentially doing the same to ourselves, because it is bound to come back to us in some form or another. For no reason should we put ourselves in predicaments that will require us to live outside the *universal code of ethics* that apply to all. We must live as such that the truth must be spoken at all times. That denotes true love of self!

Love of self demands that you practice what you preach. This means that you must stand by every word you utter. Unfortunately, most of what we see from modern-day humans is the disgraceful behavior of preaching one thing and doing another. This is done to a great extent that in some cases they enact the exact opposite of what they preach. Humans are inherently not meant to live that way! The inconsistent behavior of some is painfully apparent as they adorn superficial physical tools in an attempt to cover the stain of their souls. As it is, the "game of cons" is now the pathway to material success for the moral deviant. We see such actions in the cases of criminals who wear the most expensive suits or formal attire in the hopes that their physical appearance will deceive others as to the true decay of their person. As it is, while smiling incredulously, they harbor the most ill-mannered thoughts imaginable to humans. In observing these persons, it becomes painfully obvious that they do not love themselves. Humans are not meant to put on facades. We are all meant to be our true selves. That exemplifies true love of self.

Love of self demands that you treat others exactly the way you would like to be treated. You must give what you hope to receive. It is funny to see those who devalue others but expect respect or love in return. Such an action is a sure sign that these individuals do not understand the principles of love or simple human credos. We must not ask of others what we ourselves are not ready and prepared to give forth. Do unto others what you wish to be done to you! That is the *Law of Reciprocity* in nature.

A person who truly loves himself can easily be trusted! The trust I speak about is that which denotes that those who truly love themselves are more inclined to tread consciously and carefully in their actions, thoughts, and words. They are bound to tread aright because they are aware of a strong law and principle at play in creation: The Law of Accountability. This law is understood by many when they say, "What you sow, you shall reap." Unfortunately, most persons mistake this adage as having to do only with their actions, and as such they neglect their thoughts and words. We must come to the realization that our thoughts and words also bear consequences. One can be confident with the actions of those who truly love themselves. That is because they are aware that anything negative they enact through their thoughts, words, and actions come with grave repercussions. Therefore, they are more likely to tread aright – in accordance with the natural laws of creation.

As we come to a close on this discussion, some curious minds might wonder if loving themselves automatically means that they are predisposed to finding a suitable marital partner. Well, effectively loving oneself is a huge step towards the right direction. However, that *does not* ultimately mean that the right partner is on the other side of the door. Loving oneself and having an established self-worth is only a small step. It at least ensures that one is likely to meet with like-minded individuals. With that said, it is important to note that true love only comes as a result of a destined match and can only flourish when both parties are established in who they are.

I cannot help but to imagine how much balanced individuals will be if more persons truly loved themselves and expect the same from those around them. Alas, we are not in a utopian world, so one can only dream. However, it is not farfetched to hope that with the *knowledge of the truths of creation* more individuals will play the important role which was destined for them. If more people loved themselves, the world will be a much better place for all its inhabitants.

We must love and know ourselves so as to make our life's journey an easy one to tread. The easiest path and the unveiling of all the world has to offer begins when you are fully aware of who you are and what you are meant to do for humanity. Remember: Be thyself, know thyself, and most importantly, love thyself. That is where it all begins!

6

LOVE IN VAIN

"I LOVE YOU"

Love is a word so misused that it has now lost its real and original meaning. As it is, the gross misuse of the word has rendered it inane. It is a word many now spew aimlessly in the attempts to beguile others. It is astonishing to hear how often the masses use this word in total confidence, while their thoughts and actions towards those they profess to love indicate the total opposite. It remains unclear whether those who use this word in vain do so because they are unsure of the true meaning or that it is purposefully used because they are well aware of the power it has to elicit the many human emotions. It is almost impossible to go through a day without coming across a program on the television or reading a story based on the happenings of those who frolic around in debased acts and then turn around to those whose trust they have bridged and utter these silly words: "You know I love you, right!"

How is it possible that these misguided individuals devalue those they profess to love? Do they really love them? Or are they confused as to what true love means? In many of these cases, the debased acts of these individuals under the pretence of love borders along the lines of *hatred* towards those they so loudly proclaim to love. The word "hatred" is used in this instance because it is very apparent that the actions of these individuals illustrate a total disregard of those they continuously hurt and mistreat. As it is, such behavior is due to the lack of thorough understanding of the principles of true love, because as we all know by now, love can never serve as a tool to hurt another.

In the matters of love, as well as other natural aspects of human living, it is important to enunciate that *the totality of a human being becomes solidified when his/her thoughts, actions, and words move in complete alignment*. When there is misalignment – in which the words say one thing while the actions indicate another, we are bound to question the true intentions of that person. This is apparent in the many cases in which individuals unconsciously utter strong words such as "love" in vain.

In certain parts of the world, some have developed a culture of saying the words "I love you" almost to a fault. That now gives rise to the expectation that such words must be exchanged between persons almost on a minute by minute basis. Now, in saying that, I must clarify that there is absolutely nothing wrong with reminding those we love of the existence of such. However, the constant and expected utterance of these words without the thoughts and deeds to prove it only render such words meaningless. The utterance of this phrase without understanding its true meaning and implications speaks to the great vanity and emptiness when we use the word "love." The words "I love you" must have meaning!

VALENTINE'S DAY: A ONE-DAY AFFAIR

One of the ways that illustrate the gross vainness of love is in the way some humans subject it to a one-day affair, in what is commonly referred to as "Valentine's Day." Now, I am in no way dismissing the idea of such a day or belittling those who participate in it. The point that is being made here is that the expression of love should not be vainly trivialized into being a one-day event, in which the masses follow sheepishly in the robotic routines of buying flowers, candies, greeting cards, or going to the latest movie. There must be an unimpeachable meaning behind it all.

Is this day truly one for the celebration of love? Or is it simply a money making game concocted by the human brain? The vainness of this day arises as a result of the gross commercialization and monetization attached to it; which has done a great deal in devaluing its true purpose. As it is, many now have a "price tag" attached to their so-called love. Rather than following aimlessly, we must all find logic and conviction in our actions. Only then are we immune from becoming "pawns" in a grand game of chess.

We must take conscious actions in showing loved ones that they are truly appreciated and valued. However, we should not do this by simply following dogmas prescribed by another, of which we have no true conviction or understanding. Are human beings meant to be products of social conditioning? No! We must all be conscious of our actions as "free-thinking Beings" in creation. We are all unique in our own special way; therefore, we should all possess unique ways to express ourselves to those we love. As it is, many make the mistake of trying to act aright just for one day as though that encompasses the totality of love for another. The expressions of true love should be *year-round* in our thoughts, actions, and words towards our loved ones. *Every minute of our earthly existence should be defined by love.*

THE WORD "SEX"

There is no clearer case of the word "love" being used in vain then when it is used to describe or mean something else. Through the numerous popular movies and songs, many have come to believe that the word "sex" is synonymous with "love." That is the case because all the images shown when one professes to love another are usually of the sexual nature. As a result, many persons have developed the habit of intertwining the use of both words. This is done to a great extent that to now profess to love another seemingly connotes that there is sexual intention in said words. What is most puzzling is that many of the "love singers" who promulgate such messages do not know what they speak of. All this now produces is a classic case of the blind leading another blind.

The idea of love is much higher and sacred than that which the masses are led to believe. The sexual act is a by-product of true love. It serves as only a *small part* of the many elements under true love shared by two mature persons. The fact that some choose to selfishly manipulate the meaning of the word "love" into something sometimes defined by gross turpitude does not in any way alleviate the fact that true love stands for what it is. The attempts to adopt and morph the use of words to suit our selfish needs will only lead to more heartache and suffering – as evident in the world today.

RELIGIOUS FANATICS

In speaking of the gross misuse and misappropriation of love, *Religious fanatics* take the cake. As it is, many of these persons enact destruction and carnage under the proclamation of the love for their God. How absurd! What is even more appalling is the fact that most take these actions based on thorough conviction in what they do. In observing such actions, it is painfully apparent that these persons have been greatly deceived, as they blindly follow ideologies set forth by "tools of demons" in human form, who intend to pit human against human in the *great fight for nothingness*. And as it is, many remain blindly entrenched in the "unending war of ideologies." Why must our different ideologies be the basis on which we take up arms against each other? Such actions do not denote love of self, or of the "One" they claim to serve.

I implore these persons to ask themselves this question: What do I really gain from destroying another? It should be apparent to those who are honest with themselves that absolutely nothing is gained from such acts. If they are honest with themselves, they will come to the realization that they are more enthralled and encumbered by the workings of an evil entity, and not in accordance with the workings of the Supreme Being who created all. Alas, to come to such realization, they must rid themselves of old teachings and habits which act as a blockade to logical reasoning.

True love of the Creator demands that humans abstain from destroying all which He has created. True love of the Creator is in adhering to the natural Will; which does not constitute the attempt to destroy another. The act of destroying another is solely the concoction of the diseased human brain, and *must not* be misconstrued as an ordination from the One they claim to serve. Those who destroy under the claims of love for the Creator will have much to bear!

Now, in light of the foregoing, many might ask: "Must we be permissive to the trampling of others under the claims of love?" The answer to this question is an emphatic No! Doing so does not denote love of self. The only case in which individuals are justified in acts against another is when they are unjustly attacked, or in cases in which another infringes on their natural given right to be. In such cases, they must employ measures of "*self-defense*" and self-preservation. It must be emphatically stated that the act of subduing another in an attempt to defend one's existence must come as the absolute *last resort*, when there is no other alternative. We must defend and preserve that which has been granted to us. Only fools will allow another to trample on them unjustly.

FALSE LOVE AND AFFECTION

One of the greatest ways humans utilize love in vain is by subjecting it to a game. This is displayed by the acts of those who frolic from one venue to the next in the hopes of serendipitously finding what they perceive to be love. That is a far cry from what was originally intended for humans! What many of these individuals claim to seek is someone who will love them unconditionally and shower them with affection, and in the hopes of accomplishing this, they sell their rights to make wise decisions. What they should be more concerned about is whether the individuals they seek were truly meant for them. It is important to note that seeking love from another who is not a destined marital partner will result in a limited show of affection, which lacks the feelings and emotions of true love, because the feelings and emotions attached to true love are inherently fulfilling.

In the misunderstanding of love, many misconstrue and define a show of affection by another as love. It is true that the show of affection is an important element of true love because it serves to reiterate to a loved one that they are appreciated. However, we must realize that the mere appearance of affection does not necessarily denote love. In some cases, the show of affection might only mean that there is a fondness for someone. It is important to make this distinction because many fall under the spell of thinking that an individual loves them simply because they are affectionate. If such affection does not come as a result of a firm foundation of true love, then it was probably only meant to foster a friendship and nothing more.

Now, with that said, some might be inclined to ask if affection can grow to become full blown love. To answer such a query, it is important to clarify that affection or the show of affection is a by-product of the love that exists between two persons. It does not automatically mean that individuals are meant to be in a relationship or union, especially without the foundation of true love. The show of affection should not be used vainly as a means of trying to "buy love" from another. The show of affection must not be used as a way to influence another in the hopes that they will magically develop an attraction or affinity that is not inherently existent. Doing so will be detrimental, especially if there is no natural affinity or reciprocal feeling. *True love can only flourish when there is mutual affinity for one another.*

The idea of vainly trying to purchase affection is a sure sign that true love does not exist. We should not get into the habit of trying to *buy love* from another. That can only produce false love and affection. The attempts to buy love generally leads to the numerous complaints by those who do so that they were "jilted by love." Those who make such complaints must realize that they were not jilted by love. It is all too apparent that they were jilted or hurt by that which they misinterpreted to be love. In the cases in which true love exists, no party will consciously attempt to jilt or hurt the other.

Further, in assessing true love, we must note that *what was meant to be will be.* When we look at those with whom we share strong bonds, namely the parent-child and sibling relationships, it is very apparent that the show of affection is a natural action which is not forced by either party. This is so because it is an inherent part of the bond they share. The same logic applies in the cases of those we perceive to be potential partners. As a result of the natural love that both parties share, the show of affection only serves to reinforce that which is inherently established.

There are no two ways about love! It should be the driving force of all we do, because this was how we all came to be and how we subsist. Love is what it is. Anything we do that is not in accordance with the principles of true love cannot be justified under the shroud of love. In the matters of love, we must say what we mean and mean what we say. Ergo, we must stop the habit of using love in vain!

7

THOUGHTS, WORDS, AND ACTIONS

Our thoughts, words, and actions speak the absolute truth as to all we harbor within! In preceding discussions, many may have noticed that I briefly touched on the concept of our thoughts, words, and actions. Well, in this chapter I shall elaborate further. Our consciousness as breathing and living Beings strongly necessitates that we are all aware of our thoughts, words, and actions. But more importantly, we should be aware of how they all play a very important role in shaping our environment.

Now, some might wonder: What is the connection between our thoughts, words, actions and the concept of love? That is a very good question. The answer is that they are all greatly interconnected! These three elements have everything to do with our experiencing as conscious Beings, of which love is an important part.

Our actions and words are the physical enactments and manifestations of our thoughts. Therefore, whenever we talk about love, all three elements are of paramount importance. In the larger picture, only when all these elements are taken into account can we truly assess the intentions in all we do. As such, it is clear to see that the contradictions in our thoughts, words, and deeds remain a major reason why many suffer in the name of love.

INTENTIONS

In the early discussions, I talked about the impulse or *driver* for love as being very important in gauging our feelings towards someone, as the driver points to the greater rationale of why we feel as we do. Now, in the case of these three elements, our *intention* is the greatest determining factor in all we do. *Intentions in deed tell all!*

The intentions in all our actions speak to the great impulse of why we act. If all is right, our actions should not contradict that which we utter or think. There are those who claim to love another but take ill-intentioned actions towards them. How can that be? If our intentions in deed are not pure, then true love does not exist. The fact that there is gross contradiction in the lifestyles of some persons indicates that there is a mistake in their understanding of the words they utter, or even worse, that there is a gross disregard for them. This speaks to the larger fact that there is great disengagement between the thoughts, words, and actions of some individuals. Now, when we speak of our intentions, it all starts with the thought.

THOUGHTS

Thoughts are a very powerful element because they are the *seeds* that eventually lead to our actions. When the foundation of a relationship or union is set aright, we can only generate pure and positive thoughts towards those we truly love. It is inconceivable that anyone who truly professes to love another can harbor ill-minded thoughts towards them. If such is the case, then it becomes very apparent that the feeling defined as love is in fact something else. Many individuals take their thoughts towards others for granted, and this is largely because they wrongfully assume that only their actions bear consequences. Nothing could be farther from the truth!

Our "thought process" is actually a form of energy that emanates from within the core of a human being. It is a fact that many are confused about thoughts, and such confusion is understandable. This confusion is illustrated by those who ask: "Where do our thoughts come from?" Our thoughts generate from the core of our consciousness. In essence, the human being is in charge of his/her thoughts. This is why it is impossible to generate conscious thoughts while we are at sleep. During sleep, our consciousness is not fully at play, therefore the mind is unable to engage in the process it takes to develop a thought. This form of energy is a grace and gift to humans which was meant to help formulate and sow seeds which would eventually be enacted for the betterment of all humanity. However, in some cases, what we see today is the dissipation of our thought energy in wrong forms, consequently manifesting in destructive actions.

In an individual's thought process lies the essence of the true person. What that simply means is that it is possible to determine the potentials of any individual simply by the way he/she thinks. *Tell me how an individual thinks, and I can safely tell you who he/she truly is!* The way individuals think is highly indicative of their capabilities, potentials, and how they view the world around; as such, it is possible to envisage what they can enact for humanity.

The thought is a vision to the innermost workings of humans. All we enact starts from a single thought in the mind. Since the beginning of humanity as we know it, many of the outstanding inventions and artistry enacted by humans, which stemmed from the hopes to make the world a better place for its inhabitants, began with a single thought in the minds of those who were open enough to receive. It becomes clear that the thoughts of these people could have only come from the depths of that which is pure and unadulterated.

Many of these individuals were well aware that their thoughts are very powerful and useful, for they knew that if used aright, it can serve as a tool to help us unlock the tremendous potentials that all humans innately possess. This shows that all humans should strive to be in tune with their inner Being. In doing this, they are likely to find and harness their special gifts. Now, imagine the great possibilities for humanity if we all were to consciously tap into our inner self and do the works we were meant to do. Oh, what a world that would be!

There are some men and women who proclaim to be in a committed relationship but engage in the practice of conjuring unhealthy and lustful thoughts for another. How is such possible? Most are bold enough to say that all they are doing is thinking and not acting, therefore there are no repercussions because they assess that no one was harmed. Surely they are just thoughts, right? Wrong! *True love of another with whom we are in a committed union or relationship must be absolute in our thoughts, words, and deeds.* It is pointless to claim to "look but not touch." That is a sign of gross incontinence and selfishness. Why fantasize about another if your union is inherently fulfilling? Doing so indicates that the union lacks something. In the cases in which a union or relationship is not fulfilling, both parties must part ways. Any union or relationship defined by true love will lack nothing. As such, there will be no reason whatsoever to harbor lustful thoughts for another.

Is it possible for our thoughts to be harmful? Some perceive our thoughts to be an abstract form which lacks substance, and as such, they cannot materialize or that they have no physical implications on humans. This assertion is absolutely wrong! Nothing in nature goes to waste. When we assess and study the many destructive humans of the past and present, it is apparent that a common characteristic of all these individuals is in the way they think. It all lies in their thought process. What differentiates these people from the average positive thinking human being is the fact that they consciously and continuously nurture pernicious thoughts; at which point the only option is to resort to action. We must realize that the process of simply harboring a negative thought comes with the grave potential that such thoughts will be acted upon. Therefore, we must all learn to consciously think aright. *True love of oneself and others demands that we must not consciously or unconsciously foster any evil thoughts.*

Now, some might wonder if it is possible to "sometimes" harbor ill-intentioned thoughts about those we claim to love. Well, needless to say, the answer is an emphatic No! In the cases of true love, it is virtually impossible to consciously harbor ill-intentioned thoughts towards another. Not even sometimes! Granted, now and then a loved one is bound to upset us at some point in time, and if that occurs, the automatic response will *never* be to hurt them or mistreat them. With the existence of true love between parties, the only natural inclination is to send positive and uplifting thoughts. If that is not the case, then we must reevaluate that which we claim to be love.

The fact that our thoughts sow the seeds of which all actions generate spells that all humankind must be aware when seeking a potential marital partner. We must ensure that there is a *strong alignment in the way both parties think*. Now, an alignment in the thinking process does not mean that both parties must think identically. What it means is that they should have a common frame of thought. As such, there is bound to be commonality in ideology. In light of that, some might also wonder if it is possible to maintain a harmonious union in cases in which both parties are polar opposites in their mode of thinking. The answer to such a query is a resounding No! It is impossible for individuals who do not possess a common frame of thought to commingle in a harmonious union or relationship. Such is actually unfathomable because the idea of being in a union with another comes with the implication that both parties are of a similar mindset. The popular notion that "opposites attract" is a great fallacy when we talk about the way individuals think. *When we assess our mode of thinking, only like must attract like!* Any deviation will produce grave results.

Having a relationship or union in which both parties think differently on the important issues in life will only lead to confusion. In many of these cases, some of its participants are bound to wonder why the other party acts the way they do. Well, the answer is simple! It is simply because both persons think differently. In a relationship or union in which both parties are on the same page, such puzzlement will be nonexistent because the thinking and rationale behind all their actions will come from the same place. A key point of note in maintaining unions or relationships with individuals who are of a similar mindset is that there will always be consonance in all they do. The relationship or union will flow seamlessly. A commonality in thought speaks to the possibility of both parties pursuing similar goals in life; and such can only lay the groundwork in which individuals can understand and better communicate with each other. Sometimes the commonality is so great that they can even communicate without having to utter a word.

Flipping the coin, it is important to note that the enormity of negative thoughts can also be the breeding grounds for individuals with similar destructive intentions to meet and possibly enact that which they think. Sadly, many are hampered by the hollowness of their thoughts, consequently making them susceptible to the *cumulative negative thought banks* concocted by the human mind; and as a result, they can be driven to negative and destructive actions. Those who have allowed themselves to be encumbered by negative thoughts must learn to *consciously think aright*. Only then do they exclude themselves from the influences of negative thoughts created by others. Alas, this must be a conscious decision on their part. On the other end, there are the many cases in which individuals who are truly loved by those around them are steered in the right direction to fulfill positively for humankind. The *positive cumulative thoughts* towards these individuals have the potential to greatly influence them – if they strive to be good and are open to receive.

The importance of our thoughts is such that the preponderance of a common line of thought by the majority in a specific environment can swell up to take on form and greatly affect those involved accordingly. The best example of such happenings is when we look at the voting systems in *truly* democratic societies.

Since these societies operate under the credo that the desires of the majority are to take effect, before the physical act of going to the polling places and punching in ballots, the majority must all have a common frame of mind, which stem from the thoughts of the citizens. As such, the act of voting is only the physical manifestation of that which started from a thought. That spells the importance of a thought! Please remember this: *We control our thoughts, our thoughts do not control us!*

WORDS

Words help us convey that which we think and feel. In the material world, it is the ability to communicate with one another. The essence of words is that they must have meaning. Why some individuals speak the opposite of that which resides in their thoughts remains a great puzzle! The cry of many humans who suffer under the hands of those who supposedly love them is as a result of the great contradictions in their words. This outcry is very telling, because it tells us that humans are inherently aware of this fact: *When there is true love between parties, the words we speak will never be used as a tool to hurt or mistreat another.*

How can individuals use words as a tool of combat against those they claim to love? Well, the answer is very simple! It simply tells us that there is great confliction in the way these individuals think and act. In other more severe cases, it could be that they are well aware that there is no heartfelt emotion towards those they claim to love, and this is expressed by using hurtful words. It is important to always keep in mind that *when there is true love, our words will only serve to uplift each other.*

As it is, there are those who consciously use words as a means to deceive others. In this "game of deceit," they consciously utter powerful words solely to get something from those whom they do not really love. For some, words are now simply a way of trying to outwardly justify that which they know is nonexistent. The mere utterance of words which we do not feel or mean is bound to bring grave consequences. We must only utter "true words." Our words must stem from the core of our Being. We are all bound by our words; therefore, we must not speak fecklessly. If not heartfelt, we must not utter it. Silence is the key! *Let your words hold meaning!*

ACTIONS

Actions are the most obvious medium in which humans communicate a message. Of all the three elements, it is the most apparent because our actions can be seen and felt. It would be naive to assume that many do not understand the power of their actions, because as it is commonly said: "Actions speak louder than words." When we truly love another, it must not just be said, it must be truly meant and enacted in actions that serve to show such love.

An individual who proclaims to love another but turns around and takes actions to physically hurt and mistreat that person is greatly misinformed about his/her true feelings. The inherent feeling of truly loving another makes it virtually *impossible* to even harbor the slightest thought of doing anything to hurt that person. In looking at the misguided actions some take under the guise of love, we see the many cases of those who delve into taking physical actions to harm those they claim to love. This is sometimes done with the selfish notion that since they profess to love the other party, said party now belongs to them and no one else. It is all too apparent that these individuals are encumbered due to the great level of delusion that blinds them to reality. And to make matters worse, some of these despicable crimes committed in the guise of love are categorized as "crimes of passion," which certain justice systems in the world seem to justify under the premise that such crimes involved little or no premeditation. What an abomination!

Though there are those rare instances in which an individual must instinctively subdue or disarm another in *self defense*, we must keep in mind that many of the acts of humans stem from a thought. Therefore, it is very clear that there is some element of premeditation in the actions we take. The conscience of humans was given to help dissuade us from acting on such thoughts, as *the conscience is the bridge between our thoughts and actions.* Whatever formulates in the human mind must pass through this bridge. Therein lies the ultimate decision of what is *right* or *wrong*. As such, the question of how much time was used in the planning and premeditation of such acts is highly irrelevant. The fact that an individual has consciously decided to harm another under the pretence of love is reason enough to prosecute at the highest level, without baseless and silly considerations. Needless to say, the act of harming another denotes hatred not love. True love demands that if it is assessed that a mistake was made in trying to build a relationship where there was no foundation to build on in the first place, the only recourse is to move on and allow the other party to do the same as well. *True love is freedom. We must let our actions positively reinforce that which we think and say!*

FREE-WILL

Our thoughts, words, and actions combined are greatly related to the *free-will* of humans. As it is in nature, all humans are blessed with the ability to be free-thinking and acting Beings. A great attribute of humans that differentiates them from the animal kind is the fact that they were granted free-will. As we know, animals operate largely by instinct, of which there is no sophisticated form of thought, because they spring into action largely by impulse. On the other hand, humans possess an innate ability to think things through before embarking on any action. It is unfortunate to see that some individuals do not use this ability in the right ways, or worse, they just do not use it at all.

Some believe that through their free-will they can think, speak, and act as they please. Some even believe and assume that the free-will granted to them is a license or passport to travel into the great depths of turpitude and beyond. But no! These beliefs are wrong and unfounded! Continuing with such beliefs is bound to lead many down the road to unending suffering – as is evident in the happenings in the world today. What some of these persons fail to realize is that the grace of free-will comes with utmost responsibility, for there is a stipulation attached. The stipulation is very simple: If we go against the laws of creation, we are bound to suffer.

The concept of free-will might produce a conundrum in the minds of many, because it seems to be an oxymoron. I reckon that many may ponder how it is possible that our free-will is in fact "not free." Well, we must be cognizant of the fact that free-will is not a decree to humans to freely explore all they have been given in a negative and destructive manner. It comes with the utmost expectation to be used aright in all that is uplifting for humanity. Not doing so will only breed dire repercussions. Although free-will was meant to be a grace, some have turned it into a curse, as they have used it to their detriment.

Under the guise of seeking love, certain individuals have adopted the practice of fornicating uselessly around town under the impression that such acts lack punishment, because they perceive that they are free to experience. Well, they have another thing coming! What these persons fail to realize is that anything negative formulated by a human bears grave consequences. We must account for all we enact in creation.

For better understanding, the idea of free-will could be likened to the concept of a driving license. The provision of this license gives the holder the privilege to drive, which enables him to accomplish various goals. As we know, the granting of this license comes with the expectations that the holder must adhere to the rules of the road. Now, if for any reason the license holder chooses not to abide by the rules of the road, the license – the right to drive freely – will be revoked. As such, the freedom to use the license and its privileges was turned into a curse, though it was not meant to be that way.

Now, as we come to a close on this discussion, here comes the ultimate question: Will positive thinking, speaking, and acting bring true love? The answer is No! The point of purifying your thoughts, words, and deeds must not be done with the selfish attempt to "find love." Doing these things should symbolize true love of oneself. Remember, if we do these things with a selfish intent, our intentions are not pure; therefore, the results might not be propitious. With that said however, it is important to keep in mind that only in thinking, speaking, and acting aright are we open to attract those who are alike. It is an unattainable goal to expect to attract an upstanding individual when one is not such. It is therefore advised that all conscious Beings think, speak, and act aright!

When we assess our thoughts, words, and actions, it becomes very apparent that the completeness of a human being is only attainable when these three elements are in strict accordance and alignment with each other. It is advised that all individuals consciously create an alignment in all they think, say, and do in their daily lives. Normalcy of human behavior denotes that our thoughts, actions, and words must all flow in the same direction.

True love demands that you must only harbor positive thoughts toward those you love. Your words should serve to express that which is in your thoughts; and your actions will further serve as the physical manifestation of such thoughts and words.

8

IS LOVE CONDITIONAL?

Is love conditional? This is the ultimate question. The notion of unconditional love implies that we are to love another without bounds, parameters, considerations, or conditions. There is the general belief by many that love in its true essence is unconditional. Could that assertion be true? Well, ideally, that would be the case. However, in the material world, this is not the case. One key to unlocking the truths of love is to openly assess those who are truly worthy of unconditional love. The most important question in assessing the conditionality of love should be: Is everyone worthy of unconditional love?

In the matters of love, it is important to assess the conditions and parameters that are attached to those who are worthy of it and those who are not. *Not everyone is deserving of unconditional love!* I am sure that this statement may sound appalling to some because it goes against "conventional wisdom." Well, if the adherence to conventional wisdom takes many down the road to undue pain and suffering, it is only logical that we must reassess these generally accepted belief systems. Only in doing so will the truth be unveiled!

In most cases, the general belief that love is unconditional only fosters the persistence in unhealthy and disharmonious relationships. And as a consequence, it becomes apparent that when many say they love someone, there is the tendency to become totally engrossed in extreme blindness. This blindness now lays the grounds for unhealthy unions and relationships, which only serves to denigrate them. That is not what love was meant to be for humankind!

The unconditional belief of love denotes that we can sacrifice ourselves for the happiness or contentment of another even when it is painfully apparent that these individuals do not reciprocate such feelings. What is more puzzling is that many subject themselves to becoming victims of others by uttering such an unconscious phrase like: "If I didn't love you, I would leave you." This is in essence love in vain! What these individuals forget to ask themselves is whether those they profess to love are truly worthy of their love. The self-sacrifice to those who have proven unworthy is the breeding ground for the many persons who become *"victims of love,"* or to be more precise, they become victims of what they perceive to be love.

In assessing our various relationships, here is a question I encourage all readers to think about: Is it possible for anyone to say without hesitation that they love those who are inimical to their progress and happiness? After conscious cogitation, if anyone can provide an affirmative response, then it is very clear that they lack a thorough understanding of the principles of true love and what it means to truly love oneself and another. The feelings they might have towards those who stand in the way of their progress could be best defined as a strong fondness and affinity, or perhaps, dependence. Such feelings should not be misconstrued as love. *Love for another requires that we hold them to the highest standard and should not expect anything less.* When an individual stands in the way of our *positive* movement, it is painfully apparent that they do not support our progressive aspirations and actions. As such, we are bound to question where such a relationship stands. *True love does not hinder the progress of another.*

The love many individuals share can be easily severed and strained when they become virtual enemies because one stands in the way of the progressive movement of another. On that account, it is important that *we only show love to those who are worthy to the loved. We must only love those who love the light and consciously strive for positive growth.*

As it is, the adherence to misguided ideology has led to the enormity of cases we see on a daily basis, in which many individuals participate and remain in disharmonious relationships under the guise of love. In these unhealthy relationships, they utter silly phrases like: "I only bear your nuisance because I love you," or "If we didn't have kids, I would leave you," or "I am only in this relationship because of this or that." What preposterous things to say! Do these words constitute true love for another?

Through such words it is all too clear that these persons have attached "mundane conditions" to their so-called love for each other. It quickly becomes apparent to a conscious observer that all that exists between these individuals is simply the unmistakable semblance of love, which could be best defined as "convenience." Such partnerships only persist due to an obvious tolerance for each other. The maintenance of such relationships is bound to continually foster the nonsensical behavior, and even worse, it encourages individuals to continue hurting and mistreating themselves.

To further assess the unconditional beliefs of love, let us take a look at some of the men and women who were destructive forces to humanity. These are persons who have *consciously* committed some of the most atrocious and heinous acts against fellow humans, and consequently, against themselves. Now, we should all ask ourselves if these destructive individuals are worthy of love. Can the parents, family members, and friends of these persons confidently and openly profess undying love for them? We must ask ourselves: How can we love those who enact destruction to humanity? It is very obvious that these individuals do not belong in the midst of those who strive for the betterment of humanity; therefore they must be castigated to a homogenous dwelling of like-minded persons.

If love were truly unconditional, as many believe, these individuals should be accorded the same level of love, compassion, and support as those men and women who consciously strive for the betterment of humanity. With such, it is easy to see that there are those who are unworthy of love because their actions are not in accordance with the strict principles that guide human behavior and actions. Those who consciously deviate from the code of ethics that apply to all humans have proven that they do not deserve compassion or love, and should be treated as such.

Now, some may perceive that such words are extremely harsh and unforgiving, as they might claim that these individuals have the potential of truly discovering their faults and may want to change. To that, it must be clarified that I do not speak of those who make *minor* mistakes in acts that bear no malice or ill-intent, as these are mere infractions which can be easily remedied. I am referring to those individuals who consciously and intentionally engage in destructive acts that greatly affect fellow humans.

These are enactments that cannot be easily rectified. Though there is a possibility that some of these destructive persons might claim to have changed their ways, we must keep in mind that until an individual truly repents and actively takes corrective actions to remedy his mistakes, it is unwise to trust that person.

THE CONDITIONALITY OF LOVE

When we speak about the conditionality of love, the more pertinent question should actually be: Was love originally meant to be conditional? The answer is No! Love was not meant to be conditional. In the true sense of things, in a world where all humans acted aright, true love *would not* have any conditions attached to it. This is because all thoughts, actions, and words towards each other will only serve to foster true happiness and growth. However, since we do not live in an ideal or utopian world, there now must be conditions attached to those who are worthy of our love and those who are undeserving. These conditions come in play as a result of the wrong and destructive actions that certain humans decide to take upon themselves and to others around them.

The conditions attached to those we choose to love apply to all persons, whether they are family members, spouses, or friends. *Love is a choice and a decision!* It is a decision all persons must make as to who is worthy of their love and who isn't. In light of this however, I must emphatically state that *there are those who are worthy of unconditional love*. This is because they have proven overtime that they are worthy of one's love, and they must be treated as such. *Unconditional love can only be shown to those who have proven worthy of love by their actions, thoughts, and words.* Therefore, it is imperative to only associate ourselves with those who strive for the betterment of humanity.

As we know, true love constitutes having a healthy respect for one another. Respect for those around us is one way of showing them that they are appreciated. As humans, we are all bound to make mistakes at some point in our earthly experiencing; however, it is important that we differentiate between mistakes that can be remedied and those that cannot.

Remediable mistakes occur without a conscious intention to hurt or mistreat another. Irremediable actions are those that show a deliberate attempt to put the life of another in jeopardy. These are actions that show a gross disregard for another. When such deliberate actions to hurt another are apparent, it is obvious that there is no consideration or respect for that person. In such cases it would be foolish to shower such persons with unconditional love. *It is a fool's game to claim to love those who constantly hurt and mistreat you.* If an individual has proven through their words and actions that they do not respect or value you, it is obvious that such a relationship should be reassessed, and if necessary, must be severed.

Now, in assessing this stipulation of love especially with regards to family members, some presume that we are bound to love *all* our family members as this is only natural. Well, such a presumption is true in part. As it is, there are those who believe that they can choose their friends but not family members. Many say this with the connotation that they are automatically bound to love their family members because they do not have a choice otherwise. To that, it is important to note that the fact that individuals are family members or share the same family lineage does not automatically mean that they must love each other.

As it is apparent in the world today, there are many cases in which many persist in unhealthy relationships with family members under the claims of love. In some cases, these relationships only persist due to tolerance for each other. That is not the way to live! If a family member strays from the path of positivity, it would be unwise to indulge them under the claims of an "obligatory love." We are not in any way obligated to love anyone with whom we do not flow harmoniously! For true love to exist and grow, all parties must trust and respect each other. If such trust and respect does not exist, we are bound to live in disharmony. That is not true love! *True love is defined by harmony!*

In assessing marital unions, it is an unassailable fact that these relationships exist under strict conditions which we must live by. If these conditions are breached, then the love between parties can cease to persist. Mind you, I must clarify that these conditions I speak of are not the mundane and superficial considerations that some might ascribe to. Rather, I speak of the core virtues on which a union is built – trust, respect, commitment, etc. If for any reason one party takes the other for granted, then a condition on which the union was set is broken.

Now, let us take a look at one instance of human living which has turned many into victims of love. In the marital vows, many confidently pronounce their ties to each other by the saying: "For better or worse." This saying connotes that they are bound to a relationship even if one party devalues the other. As it is, the blind adherence to this vow has propelled so many into becoming "slaves of love." If by saying "worse," these persons are talking about the factors that are beyond the control of humans which they might experience, then they are right. However, if when they use the word, they are speaking of conscious feckless decisions and actions by one party to devalue the other, then they are absolutely wrong. The "worst" thing that can happen in a union is the conscious mistreatment and devaluation of the other. When one party consciously mistreats the other, true love cannot persist! Those who hold on to *"dead unions"* under the belief that they must persist even when another has acted in ways to greatly devalue them only do so to their detriment. The adherence to misguided doctrines is a pathway to undue suffering!

The most important condition with regards to love is that we must not allow another to take us for granted in the name of love. This simply means that love, or the misguided perception of love, should never be used as an excuse or justification to allow another to devalue us. In allowing that to happen we denigrate ourselves. That does not denote true love of self. With that said however, it is important to note that in the cases in which a union is built on the foundation of true love, this condition will *never* come to play. Those who truly understand the principles of love will never act in ways to consciously take another for granted!

In light of what we have touched on thus far, it is all too clear that due to the belief that love is unconditional, many persons persist in destructive and unhealthy unions and relationships in the name of love. *Love must not be a tool to foster pain, unhappiness, and suffering.* Persistence in such loveless relationships is unadvised! It is advised that we end such relationships. We must not blindly persist in that which does nothing to ennoble the mind, body, and soul. The choice of whom to love is ours to make. We must choose wisely!

9

LUST VS. LOVE

Are individuals perceived by many as comely and physically attractive more deserving of love as opposed to their so-called unattractive counterparts? Although the answer to this question should be very obvious, it is meant to serve a purpose. This question goes a long way in helping provide the difference between true love and lust. To a conscious observer, it is all too clear that what drives some individuals in the pursuit of so-called "good looking" persons is merely lust coated with the unmistakable semblance of love. Sadly, many now comfortably misconstrue their feeling of lust for another as love. As it is, a huge proportion of those who now claim to be "in love" are only truthfully "in lust." This spells the great battle of "Lust vs. Love."

It is very interesting to witness the sometimes vigorous discussions and arguments that go on in certain circles about which element should come first on the road to love: lust or attraction. In these debates, some ascribe to the notion that lust comes first and then the attraction develops, while others think it is the other way around. Now, it is even more interesting that some in the scientific world have a say on this topic. They attempt to define lust by

121

analyzing the various body chemicals that are apparent during what they claim to be "lustful episodes." Well, I do not doubt that such reactions happen. But what we must realize is that the study of the body's reaction to a feeling that might be unhealthy – if directed towards the wrong persons – does absolutely nothing to help the development and advancement of humankind as a whole.

What we should be more concerned about is whether this lustful feeling is in accordance with the natural path humans were meant to follow. It is important that we ask ourselves this question: If lust is a natural path to building a *love defined* relationship, will the love persist when the concupiscence wears off? As a consequence of not asking this question, it is apparent why so many people become *victims of lust-driven relationships*, as they sometimes attempt to employ all tricks known to humans to maintain "dead relationships."

The greatest misinformation on the concept of lust comes from those who present themselves as love experts or gurus. Many set up shop with the sales pitch that they can make anyone fall in love, or that they can teach strategies to make another fall into an uncontrollable lustful state for their clients. To make matters worse, their selling point is that they possess esoteric knowledge only known by a selected few. There is no fitting word to express the gravity of the deceitful and misleading information these persons spew into society.

Through their teachings, some individuals are conditioned to believe that they must employ all means necessary to keep another at a heightened state of lustful longing for them, and this will surely lead to a long-lasting union. What these "experts" forget to tell their clients, or comfortably omit, is what will happen after the lustful state wears off – as it always does. Perhaps they hope that by the time the concupiscence dwindles down love would have developed. Wow, nothing could be more wrong!

It is sometimes funny to read the teachings of the so-called love gurus, who advocate that in the process of courtship certain parties – most often women – should set a definite time period of sexual or lustful withdrawal, in which afterwards they are free to engage in intercourse with prospective partners. Some advocate a "three-month rule," some encourage six months, while others advise a longer waiting period. And all this is done with the hopes that the longer the "hold-up," the other party would become much more enraptured in an uncontrollable lustful state for them, and the lustful longing will surely lead to love. Now, here is a question for cogitation: What stops the other party who is aware of this hold-up rule to curb himself while he patiently waits for the silly trial period to reach its expiration date? As a result of many not asking themselves this question, we get to see the actions of individuals who go a lifetime employing one three-month period episode after another with numerous partners. And sadly, this is done to almost an uncountable point. Through this we get the multiplicity of those who feel duped by persons they felt would eventually love them, all thanks to the love gurus.

In order to understand the implications of lust-driven relationships, we must ask: Is there a connection between love and lust? To fully address this question, it is important to provide the common or general definition of lust. Lust is commonly defined simply as "an intense sexual desire or longing for another." As it is, there is the wide belief that lust for another is a healthy part in the process of building a relationship that could lead to love. Well, to that, we should ask ourselves yet another question: Is it possible for any connection *solely* driven by lust to develop into a relationship or union based on true love? The answer is No! If the driver – the gauge as to the reason we claim to feel love or attraction towards another – stems from meaningless concupiscence shrouded in the selfish desires to satisfy *soulless pleasures*, then it is all too clear where such a relationship lies, as well as the potential outcome. Such a relationship is bound to fail. Or it would remain as long as the lustfulness persists and will certainly dissipate thereafter.

To put this simply, the physical needs of anyone can only last a short time in their lifespan; what remains unshakable and unswervingly strong is the core of the person. Lust or the physical desires for another *can never* help to keep or maintain a longlasting relationship or union. We must keep in mind that the "natural physical yearning" only deals with one aspect of the total scope of what a true relationship should be. We could think of it as the tenth element in a twelve element program. If we bypass all other elements to get to this tenth element, we in turn bypass the most important elements; and in doing so, we set ourselves up for grave failure. There is the likelihood that anything could happen to the physical body which could affect the possibility of satisfying the so-called uncontrollable physical desires of human beings. So what happens in that case? Do we then run to the next available candidate to lust after?

This now brings up the cases of those who run from person to person because they are driven by lust and an insatiable longing. This is done by those who engage in promiscuous actions under the guise of being "single" and free to experience their lustful desires to the fullest. Some even have the audacity to define their actions as "love affairs." With such a definition, it is very clear that they are deluded, because all they engage in are *lust affairs*. Sadly, in most cases, they persist in this behavior under the stupendous notion that they are at an age when it is necessary to "sow their wild oats." It remains puzzling as to what they expect to find in the grand parade of worthless acts that not only diminishes their purpose in creation but greatly bears severe and dangerous consequences. Has it ever occurred to these frolicking masqueraders that their actions will only come back to haunt them at some point in time? In all the frolicking, what do they gain at the end of the day? Nothing! The drive for unhealthy lust will get them nowhere!

NATURAL YEARNING VS. UNHEALTHY LUST

Here is the ultimate question: Could lust be healthy? Well, the answer is twofold. The distinguishing factor is in the definition. If lust is defined as a yearning and longing for *the one* with whom an individual is in a "committed established union" based on the foundations of true love, then the answer is Yes. But, if it is defined as a sexual longing or desire for persons with whom one is not even meant to be with, then the answer is an emphatic No.

The concept of lust is only natural if and when one is in a union with a destined partner. In which case, lust could be defined as a healthy desire or yearning by parties in a *love-defined union*; and as a result, it can lead to a physical consummation and fulfillment that will exalt both parties. By this definition, the natural longing and attraction will only come in play after an established foundation, not before. As such, the union or relationship is not defined by an unhealthy concupiscence. Rather, it is a healthy and natural desire for one another. However, in order for this to happen rightly, such a union must first stand on all fronts – spiritually, mentally, emotionally, and physically. In doing this, humans cannot go wrong!

We must first build on something for there to be a dwelling place. We cannot build on nothingness and in turn expect something concrete to formulate. One of the greatest problems faced by so many is that they first attempt to build physical relations in the hopes that all else will materialize. As a consequence, sadly, some have become *slaves of their own desires.* How unfortunate! Lusting after anyone who is not your true and rightful partner is unhealthy. Unhealthy lust can only lead to improper thoughts, and these thoughts could potentially propel one into misguided, unhealthy, and irrational behavior. *True love is sanity.* In order to make the right decisions we must be sane.

Please remember this: *Lust is limited; true love is long-lasting.* The mark of true love is that it endures the test of time. Infatuation, concupiscence, and baseless attractions will certainly wear off at some point in time. Lust resides in the mind but it is lost to reality, as nothing tangible will ever be gained. An unnatural and unhealthy lustful desire for the wrong person will fail you. *True love will never fail you!*

10

THE SCALE OF COMPATIBILITY

It is sometimes astounding to notice the hollowness in which many speak of the attributes and qualities expected from a potential partner. When asked about their ideal mates, one is likely to hear responses like: "I want ....." or "I need ....." It is appalling to see how many people provide a list of grossly superficial physical attributes such as: tall, dark, and handsome; blond hair and blue eyes; brunette and brown eyes; and sometimes making reference to some protruding body parts which were meant to serve a different bodily function. With such responses, some speak as though they are in a human factory where they can draw up requirements and specifications that must be possessed by their *ideal mates*.

Sadly, in all the "wanting" and "needing" they are inattentive to persons they were *inherently meant to be with*. In assessing all this, it becomes very apparent that the basis of attraction for some individuals is solely that which lies on the surface. This is so because they focus intently on the intellectual construction of baseless and superficial considerations – most of which are generally perceived to be admirable features or qualities. In so doing, they lose themselves as they bypass the real person whilst focusing on the "fake person." This is the illusion of the physical, which ultimately leads to the "illusion of love."

Now, in all this, many might wonder how we can rightfully gauge or assess compatibility with another. In assessing true compatibility, the key is to open our eyes to the inherent parts of the individual. We must focus on the core of the Being. However, in order to achieve this, we must rid ourselves of the habit of assessing the wrong things as determinants of love. On the road to experiencing true love, the utmost degree of harmony is paramount. *True love cannot exist without strict compatibility.*

By now we are all aware of an important principle of love, which is to love oneself, and in turn, through the natural law of attractions of homogenous beings, one is more likely to find an equal match – if destined to be. However, it is not that simple, because just loving oneself is not enough. That is only the first step. In assessing whether there is full compatibility with another, it is absolutely necessary to be aware of all factors that will determine a harmonious union or relationship. This spells *the scale of compatibility*!

The scale of compatibility addresses the main components and aspects in human living that must be in place in order to build, maintain, and grow a harmonious partnership with the right person. Needless to say, these are not the basic mundane commonality factors based on superficial attributes. The goal for both men and women should be to strive for a partner of equal standing in the key components which are inherently apparent in all persons. These are aspect of the Being that will remain intact and will not fail if everything else dissipates. These components will only serve as a platform for continuous growth.

In assessing the scale of compatibility, it is imperative to delve into deeper aspects of the human being and psyche; only in doing this are we more likely to make decisions that will lead to a harmonious, long-lasting, and fruitful union. However, for this to happen, we must look beyond the material and physical appearances of humans because physical appearances can be extremely deceitful. In order to make the right decisions, we must assess the deeper *core of a Being* – their morals, values, principles, and frame of thought. These are the elements that animate the human being. In essence, these elements determine the true person.

To better understand this concept, let us look at the workings of an electronic toy. Even in this simplistic innovation there are some complexities. As we all know, the movements and actions of the toy are driven by the manipulations of a remote control system. Now, this toy is practically nothing but an immobile shell without the remote control to activate its movement. With this knowledge, why would anyone in their right senses want the immobile toy, which is practically dead? As it is, in the case of humans, the controller – the spirit – is that which animates the Being. It is the most important factor. The assessment of a potential partner based solely on superficial desires has great synonymity to the act of picking an *empty shell* with the deluded hopes that something tangible will come out of it. Alas, this is an unwise and potentially disastrous decision!

There are some key components and areas that need to be fully assessed before there is total confirmation on the path to tread. These areas are very definite and serve as a guide to many because they denote that a potential match is in complete alignment. Only through a thorough assessment of these components can a union built on the foundations of true love develop and grow into a harmonious one. These components are:

> The Spiritual Component
> The Mental/Intellectual Component
> The Physical/Emotional Component

THE SPIRITUAL COMPONENT

When we speak about two individuals being in a fulfilling harmonious union or relationship, the spiritual component takes precedence. Now, it is important to note that one of the many mistakes people make is the misunderstanding or misrecognition of spirituality as religion. For better understanding, we must create the distinction between *spirituality* and *religion*. Spirituality is the inherent part of our Being. Spirituality is an acknowledgement of who we are devoid of all earthly material considerations. It is also defined by the awareness that we are not totally of the physical; therefore, there is a Supreme Being or Creator who is the Mastermind of all we perceive. On the other hand, religion is a medium through which people choose to worship and express their spirituality. As we know, religion comes in many forms. There are Christians – those who follow the teachings of Jesus Christ, Muslims – those who follow the teachings of Mohammed, Buddhists – those who follow the teachings of Buddha, and many more.

The differentiation between spirituality and religion is very important because religion or religious activity is often misconstrued as spirituality. As it is, there are those who believe that if an individual is not a member of a specific religion, then he is not spiritual. That assertion lacks validity. The fact the some choose not to belong to a particular religious faction does not mean that they are not spiritual or in tune with their spirituality. It is important to acknowledge and respect all individuals irrespective of whichever faction they associate themselves.

A major reason why this differentiation is important is because many use religious affiliations as grounds and conditions in including or precluding those they perceive to be potential partners. Now, it is understandable that this is only natural, as they assume that there will be a stronger basis of commonality between both parties. Though they might be partly right in that line of thinking, it is important to note that this factor alone is just not enough, as there are some persons who follow sheepishly without thorough conviction in their associations with a certain religious sect.

The fact that both parties go to the same church, mosque, or synagogue for worship does not in any way mean that they are destined for one another. Although this condition might be necessary for one to find the right partner, it is important to note that a union based on the foundation of true love can only exist if *both parties wholeheartedly tread in absolute conviction rather than to sheepishly follow.* This simply means that just because an individual claims to belong to the same religious faction does not automatically set the grounds for a harmonious union. It should actually push one to query and fully understand the impetus of conviction that drives that individual.

The right spiritual stance for both parties is very important because it denotes that there is a *common frame of thought* with regards to their existence and purpose in life, as this is what largely guides our everyday experiencing. Only with such is the platform set and conducive for a relationship or union based on true love.

I am sure that many will agree with the logic that a husband and wife are more likely to live harmoniously if they tend to view their purpose in existence in a similar fashion. We do not live in a perfect world and there might be slight differences based on personal experiences, cultural upbringing, or other factors. However, if *spiritually in tune* with one another, the foundation of the union will be built on solid grounds. It will not crumble from the effects of a few earthquakes or the various tides in life, but will only be strengthened with time. A spiritual mismatch between both parties is bound to crumble as the cracks and faults will become very apparent as time goes by. A match based on total or equal spiritual alignment is one important step in building a strong relationship with a partner who is destined to work harmoniously with you.

Now, some might ask the question: If all else is right, is it possible to marry someone who practices a different religion? The answer to such a question is complex and will depend on the parties involved. However, a simple answer is Yes. This is because, as explained earlier, there is a difference between religion and spirituality. The fact that both parties have a spiritual understanding could lay the grounds for a union – if all else is in harmony. However, it is very important to bear in mind that although two persons might be spiritually in tune, the differences in religious customs and practices could create conflicts. And the persistence in a union in which both parties uphold different customs, and consequently do not have a *common spiritual goal*, is likely to breed grounds for disharmony. If that is the case, true love cannot flourish! If the differences in religious expressions become so apparent that it causes inconsonance between both parties, then the union was probably not meant to be. The key however is to know the scores beforehand and not blindly explore.

In view of this, it is not advised that individuals practice religious conversions solely to appease the needs of another. Religious conversion, if done, must only happen as a result of absolute conviction in the path one intends to tread. If it is done sheepishly, it will only lead to a false existence, which is likely to create self-discontentment, and with time might put a strain on the union. If the spiritual component is lacking in a relationship or union there is nothing to build on, hence the union is in essence baseless. *Spiritual compatibility is defined by the ultimate connectedness of both spirits. This is a connection that transcends the physical and will exalt both spirits.*

THE MENTAL/INTELLECTUAL COMPONENT

The mental/intellectual is another important component in thoroughly assessing a potential partner. At first glance, some might assume that this aspect deals with the intellectual capacity of both parties, or that it pertains to their earthly educational background or standing. That is not the case! Although erudition is necessary to navigate the world, assessing a potential partner solely on this criterion is grossly superficial.

The mental/intellectual aspect of humans appertains to our beliefs, thoughts, and understanding on that which surrounds us and the world at large. It is simply the *frame of thought* or philosophy of life about the important issues that we deal with on a daily basis. Another way to assess this is by looking at how we view and think about the world. This is where our values, morals, and principles come to play.

It is a fact that no two people think exactly alike. We are all unique Beings with something special to offer each other and the world. However, when it comes to our various relations, we must understand that *the most harmonious relationships or unions are those built on the utmost alignment of thought, reasoning, and ideologies.* When there is symmetry in our thinking and reasoning framework, we are more likely to grow and learn from each other. The small differences that may exist will not be the basis on which we strive apart. This is because there is a uniform foundation. This component is important because it is on this basis that individuals make the important everyday life decisions. If there is too much of a gap between parties, it becomes very obvious that there is no basis or foundation for a fruitful relationship or union.

To help shed better understanding of this matter, let us take a look at the issue of child bearing. When two persons come together, there is the proclivity to want to bear children – if they so decide. Now, if this decision is made, there must be a common understanding of the number of children they intend to bear. A scenario in which one party believes in having many children while the other prefers only one or non is a sure sign that there is a major difference in opinion on this particular matter; and this might be a definite sign that such a union was not meant to be. *The perfect union between parties will not require either party to make extreme sacrifices to accommodate the other.* Please be aware that the key word in the last statement is "extreme." Though we might make slight compromises while in a union with another, this should not be done to a grave point of losing oneself or one's identity. Even in a union, we all have our individual paths to chart and should understand that the *perfect union flows seamlessly when both paths converge not diverge.*

Though some might view the matter of child bearing as a minor issue, we must realize that what seems like a minor issue today has the potential to become a major one tomorrow. Therefore a common ground must be met from the inception of a union. Strict mental/intellectual commonality would mean that both parties have a common goal, and as such, there will only be slight differences, if any. Many family counselors advocate and encourage open communication in a relationship or union, this is very important because it gives one an insight on the inner workings – the thought process – of a potential partner. However, we must be aware not to take all that is presented to us at *face value*. There is that part of a person that is easily assessed when nothing is being said. That is the part we should be more in tune with.

Now, some might wonder if two individuals who differ mentally and intellectually can coexist in a harmonious relationship. When it comes to a marital partnership, needless to say, it is highly unlikely that two persons who view the world from very different spectrums could have a harmonious union because that could be grounds for continuous conflicts and disagreements. If the values, morals, and principles of both parties are different, there will be absolutely nothing to build upon.

Strict mental/intellectual compatibility is the ultimate meeting of the minds. It is a state of being in which we are absolutely confident in the ways and thoughts of another. If the fundamentals in ideologies are not similar, that will become grounds for inconsonance between parties. Granted, a few differences might be present so as to learn something new from each other, but the goal is to ensure that there is enough common ground to facilitate a strong foundation of true love, thus a harmonious union. *Utmost mental/intellectual compatibility will exalt the minds of both parties.*

THE PHYSICAL/EMOTIONAL COMPONENT

The physical/emotional component speaks largely to our physical existence and that which it encompasses. It is the easiest to assess by humans because it is largely defined by what we can perceive with our naked eyes. What many fail to realize is that it is just a façade. As emphasized previously, *a relationship or union which is solely based on the physical is superficial,* and as such, is bound to fail at some point in time. The physical is the most deceitful component of all because it is the first thing most people see; therefore their total judgment of another is sometimes based solely on that.

In light of this, many might ask: What is the importance of the physical if it seems to be superficial? This is a very good question. To answer such a question, I encourage you to think of buying a car. Now, the fact that the car has appealing exterior features should not be the sole basis on which we attempt to buy it. The idea of choosing a fully *functional* car is in assessing all its parts before you can make the right decision. With the same logic, the physical is meant to be that which enables all human beings to probe and delve deeper. The physical appearance is important simply because it is the manifestation of what radiates from within all humans. It is meant to lead us to ask the important questions as to *what animates the individual.* It is only to serve as that which indicates a potential match. It should *never* be used solely as the basis of assessing compatibility with another.

To further examine the physical, let us take a scenario in which the sole basis of a relationship or union was due to the physical attributes of another. In this example, let us assume that the main reason of attraction was the "sexy long shapely legs" of another. Now, unfortunately, as it may happen, this individual is involved in an accident that causes severe injuries to the legs, and as a result, the long shapely legs have to be amputated. Now, without the development of core foundations as the basis of this relationship, it is very obvious that it is now in serious jeopardy as the sole reason for its existence is no more. Only through a strong *immaterial* foundation will the inherent goodness enable a relationship or union to survive and prevail. This is because such connectedness is much deeper then what meets the naked eyes.

Another case we could cite is that of those who debase themselves by picking a so-called partner solely based on their financial standing and material worth. These cases are apparent when we observe those who seek "rich men or women" to take care of them. Those who make such decisions have greatly devalued themselves, and most importantly, their worth as humans. Here is an important question to these persons: What happens to the so-called relationship if the money is gone? Well, perhaps, the other option will be to seek out another rich fellow. And there is a strong probability that this strategy will yield the same results. This now puts them in the unending game of strutting their body parts as collateral whilst they seek one rich fellow after another. Needless to say, it is all too apparent that their behavior does not constitute true love for these materially rich persons, or even for themselves.

Sadly, after a long and difficult journey filled with numerous unpropitious experiences, it may become very clear to those who

are entrenched in material pursuits that without a firm establishment on the most important aspects of human living any union
based on physical appearances will eventually crumble. *Money or
financial standing should never be used as a criterion on which one is to
seek a life partner.* The results of such an action will only be disastrous! Money is grossly that of the physical, and as we know by
now, the material is only temporary. Any decisions made on this
premise will be temporary at best.

Alongside the physical component comes the emotional element of being. Our emotions are very important because they
drive most of what we do as well as the various actions we take.
A huge part of loving oneself is the ability to maintain a strong
emotional balance. For two individuals to be productive, they
must have temperamental commonality and compatibility. If the
temperaments are different, there is a strong likelihood that both
parties will struggle to maintain an emotionally balanced relationship.

Emotions could be defined as a manifestation of our inner feelings – which takes on various forms. It is that which seems to
move us whenever we feel something. Humans often make reference to their emotions whenever they proclaim to love someone.
So it is important that the feeling which triggers such an emotion
must come from the right place. Only then are we in control of
our emotions and not swayed by impure feelings.

*For a strong emotional component to exist both parties must be emotion-
ally independent.* Granted, we all have our down times, and it is
important to have those who can help us work through them.
However, emotional dependence should not be the sole purpose
of any partnership. If there is a great *emotional gap* the relationship
will suffer. Both parties must be of equal and *complementary emo-*

tional standing. This is as important as speaking the same language, both literally and figuratively. A partnership in which both parties have an emotional imbalance could be likened to a relationship in which one party speaks English while the other speaks French. Needless to say, it will be difficult to communicate effectively. *In order to have emotional harmony both hearts must speak and understand the same emotional language.*

Contrary to the popular notion that "opposites attract," when assessing the scale of compatibility, that will be a recipe for disaster. Such an assertion only helps validate unhealthy engagement in wrong partnerships. When we speak of strict compatibility, "the law of similars" takes effect. *A fulfilling relationship or union will only grow on the grounds of an attraction of similarities and positive propensities.* Nothing else will suffice!

THE PERFECT ONE FOR YOU

No one is perfect, but there is a perfect person for everyone. Thus it is highly feasible that a husband and wife can have a perfect union. The word "perfect" in reference to the union does not mean "without fault," rather, it speaks of the ultimate complementary union. With common grounds, one individual might be stronger in areas in which the other is weaker, and vice versa. As such, they can help each other grow despite whatever faults might exist; and this will happen without undue conflicts. It is important to note however that this can only happen when the relationship is founded on the right platform. It would be unwise to expect such in partnerships of incompatible forces. Unfortunately, due to an attempt to build a relationship with incompatible individuals, some persist in relationships in which they are constantly "trying to make things work." These persons must realize that *what was meant to be will never need continuous mending because it will come firmly attached.* On that account, it is important to note that *true love can never be fabricated. It is either there or it isn't.* It is that simple!

In most of the cases in which individuals try to make things work, all they hope to accomplish is to develop a tolerance for the other party under the guise of love. For no reason whatsoever should anyone remain in a situation that does not foster a harmonious livelihood. This strongly spells that we must be in tune with ourselves so as to intuitively know what was destined for us. As such, we would not have to journey in the dark with the hopes of magically figuring things out.

If it lies in our path to work with a partner in fulfilling our earthly goals, we should strive to be with one who is prepared and ready to work along the same path. In doing so, the journey through life will be a much easier one. *True love can only flourish when all the pros and cons are adequately assessed.* It is unwise to blindly jump into scenarios in the hopes of developing or manufacturing love as time goes by. That will not cut it!

Now, here is the ultimate question: Does a match on all components automatically mean that two individuals are meant to be together? Well, the answer lies within each individual. No outsider can answer that question for anyone. Individuals must truly know themselves in order to answer that question. However, a general answer is No. This is because the commonalities that are present might only mean that these individuals perhaps are meant to be friends and not husband and wife. With that said however, it is important to note that a high level of compatibility on *all fronts* indicates that these persons tread similarly, and as such, there could be a *strong platform* on which a harmonious union can be built.

A key test to objectively assess the potentials of a partnership lies in asking a very simple question. Ask yourself: If I take out all material considerations will this union pass the test of time? The main purpose of asking this question is due to the fact that we all know that the physical has the potential to fade at some point, and if that happens, is the relationship strong enough to survive. Objectively and honestly answer this question. You must not deceive yourself when answering this question. If the answer is "No," it should then be obvious that the basis of the relationship was not set on the right foundation. The key is to ensure that an affirmative response should come without any hesitation. And if that is the case, then there are strong grounds for the relationship to be a fruitful one.

The fact that two well-intentioned persons who were not meant for each other may have tried to build a relationship – based on the wrong assumptions that there was full compatibility – indicates that they did not do a good job of assessing themselves. It is likely that these individuals were only meant to be friends, and nothing more. We must realize that if we are in tune with our *intuitive consciousness*, it is unlikely that we will be led astray.

The intuitive consciousness of humans is a state in which we are wholly aware of our inherent ability to perceive that which surrounds us without thought or in-depth analysis. It demands that we as human beings are aware and consciously in tune with that part of our inner being that speaks to us. Many understand the concept of intuition with the saying "the first impression is always right." Now, although it is true that the first impression is important, it is advised to look much deeper thereafter. Assessing another only by what the surface presents is bound to mislead many into making wrong decisions, which they did not have to make otherwise.

Many might wonder if this intuitive ability is only accorded to a few enlightened persons. No, that is not the case! It is an ability that all humans should possess. The reason why some persons seem not to possess this ability is due to the fact that they have squelched it within themselves, therefore rendering it dormant. This is largely due to the overwhelming dependence on the work-ings of their intellect or the brain's capacity – which is strongly rooted in the physical – to guide them. As it is, many humans cal-culate so deeply that they have lost their ability to *know without thinking*. This lack of intuitive consciousness is what leads many into wrongly judging or assessing another as a compatible fit for a partner; and by doing so they open themselves to unwarranted experiences.

If all humans are in tune with this inherent ability, it is highly inconceivable that they would make grave mistakes in the name of love. Now, this does not mean that they will be immune from making mistakes. Rather, it simply spells that this intuitive con-sciousness will help them in making decisions that are not wholly rooted in deceitful physical appearances. With an active intuitive consciousness, we will ultimately obviate ourselves from grave pitfalls. Therefore, it is imperative that we all become aware of our *inner voice*! We must let this voice speak to us, for it will guide us in making the right decisions.

Please remember this: There are *many* persons who can pro-vide a match based on one component, as there are *several* persons who can provide a match based on two components. However, there are *few* who can provide a match on all three components. Now, these are the *special few* with whom one can build a truly harmonious union based on the foundations of true love.

The scale of compatibility should serve as a gauging tool in assessing the possibilities of formalizing a union. It is impossible to grow something solid and firm from an unstable foundation. If a home is built on a bad foundation, it is obvious that this home is bound to crumble at some point in time. Even though it might persist for a while, in time the natural forces will expose its many faults and it will come crumbling down. However, with the right foundation, this home is built to last a lifetime. This same analogy applies to our various affiliations. It is important that our relationships are based on the right foundations, thus they will withstand the test of time. Strict compatibility on all fronts will help lay the grounds for a solid foundation to build on.

On a scale of one to ten, the commonality and compatibility on all fronts must be at a level of *eight or higher*. A relationship or union defined by the utmost spiritual, mental, and physical compatibility presents a direct pathway on the road to true love. Nothing else will cut it! *We must openly see where we are going in order to get there safely. It is unwise to chart blindly!*

11

LOVE AND MARRIAGE

The greatest linkage in the minds of the masses when we talk about love has to do with the idea of marriage. This begs the question: What does love have to do with marriage? In an attempt to shed clarity on the true connection of love and marriage, we must first assess the modern-day beliefs and practices by humans.

In the minds of some around the world, the words "love" and "marriage" are antonyms. To them, these two concepts strive in polar opposition to each other. Why is such the case? Is it that those who speak negatively about love and marriage truly believe that which they speak? Or are these negative sentiments borne out of the unpropitious experiences many encounter as a result of misguided notions and beliefs? Due to the general negative opinions about love and marriage, many actually wonder if marriage is a natural aspect of human living, and more importantly, what role love plays in marriage.

It is true that in the current state of our world we are bound to question the true connection between love and marriage. This is understandable because what many see in the span of a lifetime are the actions of "jokesters" who perceive marriage and commitment as a game. As it is, we are now in a new age of "in and out marriages." And to make matters worse, there are the so-called love experts who appear on television shows, publish books, or write magazine articles geared to certain genders – mostly women, in which they promulgate messages of "how to get someone to marry you," or more appropriately put, "how to lure an unsuspecting fool into an unwanted marriage." All these false teachings are given with the hopes that they will help precipitate the occurrence of a marriage. These teachings are presented as though human beings are pawns in a chess game that can be moved at whim and must adhere to the volitions and desires of the ultimate player. However, for those who are conscious enough to see the flaws in those teachings, it does not take too long to discover that human beings are more complex.

Sadly, all the nonsensical jargon taught by these so-called love experts only help to further perpetrate the notion that marriage is a game; and in this game the "aggressors" are bound to win while the "nice guys" lose. How unfortunate! As a result, the concept of marriage has been utterly reduced to a practice in which many seek out the most desirable persons deemed eligible by public surveys. As such, the great battle is now to attain the love of these so-called "eligible persons" in the hopes of procuring a marriage. With such occurrences, it is no wonder that the "institution of marriage" remains a joke in the minds of many. Thus, it is no great surprise that many vigorously ridicule and impugn the institution of marriage as well as the role of love in it. Now, to fully understand why so many are skeptical of marriages, we must look at the general practices of humans.

MODERN-DAY MARRIAGE PRACTICES

In assessing the false practices of marriages that exist today, what is now defined as marriage is nothing more than a *civil* or *social contract* cloaked in gross vanity, in which some of the parties involved – especially the women – are more concerned with the pageantry of the wedding than the true marriage itself. The fact that marriages are now defined as the "wedding business" serves as proof that to some it is now more a business than an institution that holds great merit and importance. And unfortunately for humans, whenever anything that was meant to be sacred becomes a monetized commodity – of which many attach pecuniary value, it then loses its true essence and meaning.

Now, this does not mean that the idea of marriage itself is wrong or faulty, but, rather, that humans – as we always tend to do – have tried to circumvent it to suit our selfish needs, and for that reason we are bound to get negative results. Unfortunately, these negative experiences – due to misguided ideologies – now lead many to cry out loud about the "faultiness of marriages." Thus they complain of their "dwindling marriageability." And as a consequence, they turn to more sophisticated methods prescribed by the so-called love gurus to increase their marriageability.

There are those who are involved in what is termed a *"marriage of convenience."* To them, the idea of marriage is simply a means to an end. It is nothing more than a social agreement synonymous to the behavior of university roommates who engage in meaningless intercourse with the consciousness that their relationship lacks a solid foundation. Hence there is absolutely nothing to build on. To these persons, the word "marriage" is simply a covering or a guise to *validate* their selfish desires to fulfill their so-called uncontrollable physical needs. Through such occurrences, we encounter those who degrade and "cheat" on their so-called spouses – whom they claim to love. Now, such a behavior should not come as a surprise because to these individuals marriage means absolutely nothing. It is simply a baseless institution to dissimulate their true intentions in an attempt to foster unnatural human behavior, because to them the rationale for a marriage is a simple way to appease their indolent minds. For those who persist in marriages of convenience, love is not even in the equation.

Further along this line, there are those who view marriage as a contractual business agreement, in which some get in and out of "contractual marriages" in an attempt to gain citizenship into certain nations. In this instance, the idea of marriage to the parties involved is merely a money making enterprise which holds no significance. This practice has done a great deal in trivializing the true idea of marriage in the mind of the masses.

For some women and men, the intentions to seek out a marriage come as a result of societal comparisons. This is apparent as individuals compare themselves to persons in their age bracket, and as a result, there is the great push to seek out a marriage at all cost. Consequently, some fall into "false marriages" under the urging and encouragement of outsiders, or simply, from self-imposed pressure. In the same boat, the urge for marriage comes to some as a result of what many define as a "ticking clock." As such, they must hasten the occurrence of a marriage in order to defeat this "imaginary" clock – which only resides in their minds. On the road to unfruitful unions, some lower their bridges, standards, and expectations simply because they believe that true love eludes them; therefore they are prepared to accommodate anyone so as to procure a marriage, thus fitting into the mold.

To some persons, the idea of marriage serves as a tool to foster their so-called high social standing. To these parties, a marriage is nothing more than a mutually beneficial contractual agreement to combine forces in an attempt to further accomplish "material goals" that do absolutely nothing to exalt the spirit. Most of these cases are evident in the unions of those who classify themselves as the "cream of the society." The gross superficiality in the practices by these people will be appalling to an alien who does not understand the rationale of the stupid customs and traditions that humans have set for themselves.

These individuals put on lavish shows of gross vanity and pretentious behavior in an attempt to create worldwide attention, and of course, to potentially conjure up jealousy in the minds of rivals or adversaries, who might vow to outdo them when their time comes. It is apparent that the concept of marriage to these persons is nothing more than a public spectacle to bedazzle the audience at large. In these practices all we see are outward smiles, while the true persons are virtually died within. It is nothing more than a show for attention. All they are doing is simply keeping up appearances. What a shame!

Furthermore, to some, the drive to seek out a marriage is in an attempt to boast of having the "bigger and better thing." We see this in the cases of those who stupidly joke of having *trophy wives or husbands*. In most cases, these individuals are nothing more than thoughtless stooges or zombies who are put on public display as proof of the material success of another. Ask these persons the basis of their marriage and all they are bound to divulge are superficial responses as to what they perceive holds their marriage – outrageous sexual performances, gift exchanging, the provision of all material needs, and so on. It is all too apparent that their so-called marriage is held by nothing meaningful. The only stipulation that holds true in this union is that it persists only due to the constant showering of gifts and material possessions. In essence it is a *bought married*. This "fake marriage" will disappear when all the superficial things that hold it together come to a cessation. These persons could be best defined as nothing more than *long term prostitutes* who sell their bodies and souls for a certain price. But unlike their street roaming counterparts, they remain in this *perceived marriage* for as long as the wealth remains.

Though some might perceive my words to be harsh, I am sure that they would openly admit that I speak the truth. The truth must be told regardless of human sensitivity or their mere indolent state of being. Think about this: Why must we castigate the "street roamer" while the other is praised as an *upscale high-class* house dweller? The silly societal classifications constructed by humans to categorize themselves based on material valuations have no bearing in the grand scheme of things. These categorizations do not diminish the fact that both parties are in the same boat and will be judged accordingly.

In some cultures of the world it is the norm in certain circles for some individuals – predominately males – to believe that they are accorded the right to marry as many partners as earthly possible. What is more perplexing is the fact that many justify their actions under the coverage of religious teachings. Some naively justify this debased social behavior by explaining that their openness about having multiply wives or partners frees them from any burdens of guilt or accusations of misconduct. How appalling!

Can such arrangements be based on true love? Can these males confidently say that they equally love all their wives with no reservations? If they can affirmatively answer these questions, then they are within their free-will to explore. However, there is a surety that if such a claim is made, it lacks validity. This is because it is *virtually impossible* for any man or woman to rationalize love to various partners. Rather than on the basis of true love, in most cases, the intent to pursue and accumulate multiply wives is solely a means to announce their so-called "manhood." In other cases, it is simply a way to pronounce their material wealth to the society. In these polygamous practices there is the great likelihood for jealousy to arise, as one party might feel as though another receives more attention or affection from the patriarch. At this juncture, it is important to note that *with true love no party will act in any way to incite jealousy in the other*. If one party involved in the so-called union feels cheated and jealous, it is therefore apparent where the relationship stands.

Further along this line, some individuals view marriage solely as a means to procreate. Even worse, it is viewed by some simply as a commingling relationship, in which a woman is expected to aid a man with the domestic needs and bear children, while he is expected in turn to provide food, clothing, and shelter. In such conditions, the male is sometimes believed to be in ownership of his wife – just as one would take ownership of a livestock. As it is, the woman is nothing more than a "tool for procreation."And to make matters worse, under the misguided notion of love for their children – which in some cases is done with the best of intentions, the parents of these girls or women are major players in these deplorable acts. Sadly, these parents sometimes seek out and force their daughters into baseless and loveless marriages. How unfortunate!

Now, in light of all the scenarios, situations, and practices mentioned thus far, we must ask ourselves this pertinent question: *Are these the reasons to get married?*

To convey the great lengths to which the occurrences of unnatural human practices and behavior has led us, it is unfortunate to say that other than a paucity of marriages that stand aright, the vast majority of so-called marriages today are either grossly baseless or just plain wrong – when judged by the true definition of marriage and what it is meant to be. One might even say with confidence that less than fifty percent of the marriages we see today are built on a firm foundation. Now, where does this put the other marriages? Well, we can see the physical manifestations of wrong marriages in the overwhelming cases of *legal* divorces all over the world. There is an emphasis on the word "legal" because these are the ones that have openly pronounced their separations. There are those who persist in wrong and disharmonious unions solely because it is more convenient to do so. If all these parties were to make their divorces legally known, the true scale of the disharmonious marital epidemic will reveal itself.

For those who have listened intently, it should be apparent that all the scenarios and situations that have being mentioned thus far are sorely defined by the material or physical. They are all superficial and baseless attempts to build something on a crumbling foundation, or worse, with no foundation at all. As such, it is no wonder that the concept of love and marriage perplexes so many – which should not be the case.

It should be obvious to a conscious person that the idea and intentions of a marriage in its truest form greatly pales in comparison to the superficial modern-day practices of human beings. It is painfully obvious that many practically worship their intellect, as all their decisions come from the calculations of the brain. This simply means that many suppress the true telling of their inner voice while they make marriage a calculated event. In some cases, the worship of the intellect drowns their intuitive capacity to perceive that which assails them; and as such, they get into the wrong marriages. Why is that the case? Well, it is simply because it wasn't based on true love! If the purpose of a marriage or union is faulty, the foundation is in turn faulty. That will most certainly spell doom for the parties involved.

Now, to get to the root of the problem of why so many individuals harbor misguided notions about marriage, we must ask ourselves the most important question of all: *What is a true marriage?*

DEFINITION OF A TRUE MARRIAGE

Marriage is the stamp that seals a union between two persons. A true marriage will only serve to further enable spiritual, mental, and physical growth. If true, it is an unswerving and unshakeable bond between parties that can only help them fulfill to their utmost potential, for it is defined by the strengths of both parties. For a marriage or union to be stamped aright, both souls must be connected on a very deep and "immaterial" plane of existence.

For humans to be able to assess and judge the rightfulness of their behavior, we must first examine how it flows with the natural laws of creation. When we assess the idea of marriage in nature – as defined above, it is easy to see that if foundational

THE UNIVERSAL STANDARD OF LOVE

sound, the union of a man and woman can propel those destined for it into a greater sense of purpose; which in turn can only lead to the betterment of the couple and of humanity as a whole. It is unquestionable that marriage is a natural aspect of human living because in its truest form it is the union between a man and woman that can exalt both parties spiritually, mentally, and physically. We must also realize that the ennoblement of the human spirit comes in the totality of these three facets of human living. Without all three intact no marriage or union is complete.

Unfortunately, what we see today is the pursuit of one aspect – most especially the physical aspect – in the hopes that as time goes by all others will develop. To make matters worse, some so-called marriages even try to stand without the establishment of one of these important factors, as some try to build marriages simply by assessing another based on the potential to pass a simple commonality test. In doing so, they convince themselves to just simply "give marriage a trial." And this is done as though the institution of marriage is a game of trial and error – which it definitely isn't.

It is sad to see that some persons believe that all members of the opposite sex they encounter are "fair game" in the hopes of attaining a marriage. Unfortunately, some even go as far as to civilly marry another whom they do not love in the hopes that love will develop. This now brings up the question of whether two persons can get married in the hopes that love will eventually develop. As it is, some ascribe to the notion that humans can circumvent and manipulate natural laws to magically build something that wasn't meant to be. Now, it is important to keep in mind that the spiritual, mental, and physical connection that is emblematic of true love and a destined marriage is as such that it *cannot* be drummed up at will. It is virtually impossible to develop love when there is nothing to build on in the first place. It is either meant to be or it isn't!

Now, for clarity, I do not intend to mislead anyone into thinking that love is static and must remain stagnant. That is farthest from what I mean. Even in the truest form of love the relationship must be nurtured in order to grow. Hence we grow in love! However, it is important to note that in order for this growth to occur, there must be a foundation or basis on which we attempt to build and grow. We cannot build on nothingness!

THE NUCLEUS OF A MARRIAGE

True love is the nucleus of a harmonious and fruitful marriage. A true marriage can only stem from a foundation of true love between parties. Anything else cannot be defined as a true marriage. That simply means that without true love no marriage or union can stand! As it has been spelt in countless ways, no union will be harmonious or even justified without first establishing a spiritual connection. As we know by now, true love is void of any superficial considerations. Therefore, a true marriage must also be void of all superficial considerations. *If the basis of a marriage is shrouded in the superficial, it is destined to fail at some point in time.*

A true marriage is defined by the connectedness of equals. This equality has absolutely nothing to do with social standing. The connection I speak of transcends the physical, for it is characterized and defined by a spiritual and mental coequality. Essentially, both parties have to be on the exact same page! In a complemented union, both parties will only serve to reaffirm that which is inherent and established within them; thus continuing to support and help each other grow.

True marriages exist only between parties that are meant to be together. In essence, one could say that they were "prepared for each other." Many liken this idea to that of *"Soul Mates."* There are those who are meant to work together in fulfilling a common goal, as such they can be described as being soul mates. The idea of soul mates is greatly implied in the words. It could be said that these parties are joined and bonded by their inner person – the spirit. In the truest of cases, most soul mates or destined partners will effortlessly communicate spiritually, mentally, and physically. Such a union will only flow and grow with ease because both parties were meant to be. As such, there will be no elaborate attempts to "make things work," because they just do.

Now, many might be inclined to wonder aloud if each person has one suitable soul mate. Well, due to the fact that each individual is born with unique traits, there is bound to be another who can be the ultimate complementary force. However, with that said, it is important to note that there are *few* other persons who can also serve as complements. There is no ratio or number that can be given because each individual is unique and complex in his/her own way. However, it must be stated that the number of potential complementary partners are fewer than many might think or hope to have.

The fact that there are few persons that can complement one does not mean that an individual is encouraged to aimlessly "play the field" whilst engaging with multiply persons, in the deluded hopes that one will magically find their soul mate and *fall in love.* In the matters of love, as in all other aspects of human living, there is no magic. The idea of magic is simply an illusion of the mind. Once one meets another with whom there is a firm foundation, the need and yearning to continue the search should come to a cessation, for it is now time to build and grow with one's true partner.

ARE MARRIAGES MADE IN HEAVEN?

There are those who believe that "marriages are made in heaven," could this be true? Well, the answer is twofold. To get to the root of this quagmire, we must ask this question: What do the words "Marriages are made in heaven" truly mean? For better understanding, we must shed clarity by differentiating between what many perceive to be marriage and what a true marriage was meant to be for humanity. If by uttering those words we speak of what marriages were truly meant to be for humanity, then we are right in that line of thinking. However, if we utter those words with the beliefs of what we see in practice today, we might be wrong. The use of the word "made" connotes that such a union was predestined, and as such, no other human has the power to put it asunder, except the parties involved – largely through misguided behavior and practices. The predestination of a union serves to show that such a union was meant to stand, and will not swerve with the waves that might create tides. However, we must realize that only unions that are destined will survive such waves. Any union that is not built aright will be washed away with the tide.

In light of the foregoing, some might be inclined to ask: Does the fact that a marriage is destined mean that both parties will "*live happily ever after?*" This is essentially asking the question:

Can a marriage based on true love come to an end? Now, this is a very interesting question because in an attempt to answer it we must be aware of the modern-day considerations of human living. These considerations are: "What was meant to be," and "How we live today." The answer to the former consideration is an emphatic No, while the answer to the latter is Yes. Ideally, when a union is spiritually joined together – lacking all superficial considerations – it will remain strong for the lifespan of both parties. But in cognizance of the wrong ways of humankind, we must look at the ways we live, and through these lenses we can see that there are certain unions that were meant to be, but become dissolved by the wrong actions of one or both parties.

In view of this, many tend to ascribe to the notion that most marriages come to an end due to what is famously described as "irreconcilable differences." Is that a valid assertion? Though true in part, that is only half the story. It is very important to note that these irreconcilable differences are only a *consequence* of the real problem. *There are three main reasons why most marriages come to an end.*

The first reason is that the parties involved were inherently incompatible on all fronts. And in an attempt to build a marriage, the differences will only become more glaring as time passes. Simply put, these persons were just not meant for each other. The second reason is that though compatible on some fronts, some parties come into marriages with the great expectations that all the negative propensities they perceived in the other – which in most cases were signs of marital incompatibility – will cease after marriage. When their expectations are not met, the differences now become irreconcilable. However, the fact remains that these faults – which they chose to ignore – were there all along. The third reason is that even if a marriage is based on true love and both parties are compatible on all fronts, there remains the possibility that one or both of them might *become comfortable*, and as such, will start to take the love and commitment that is emblematic of the union for granted. This in turn might spell trouble for the marriage.

Now, with that said, it is important to note that persons who understand the true concept of love and marriage will not engage in or *allow* trivial matters to affect their union. This is because to them the connection that holds the marriage is much deeper, thus it is unshakeable. With the conscious awareness of this fact, they can only stride forward as they pull from strength to strength. The trials and tribulations many believe they may go through while married – which are largely self-imposed due to societal misgivings – become utterly negligible to those who stand in true marriages. As such, their marriage is an unbreakable spiritual, mental, emotional, and physical bond that binds both parties.

DOES MARRIAGE BRING HAPPINESS?

Here is the ultimate question: Does marriage bring happiness? It is important to note that a marriage in itself does not bring happiness. However, *a true marriage is bound to add greatly to one's happiness*. Those who think that love and marriage will bring them happiness might be deluded if they are not *inherently* happy and expect to gain happiness from a *wrong* marriage or partnership. In actuality, the engagement in a wrong marriage might result in the opposite of happiness. It is virtually impossible to be happy if one is with the wrong partner. For this reason, their marriage is bound to be filled with feelings of unhappiness and discontentment.

Where should marriages stand? Does it have to be a social affair? Though a true marriage is ordained, it does not need to be recognized by any states, governments, or countries to be validated. Such recognizance is largely inconsequential, as it is only a construct of the human intellect to keep tabs on all citizens and inhabitants of a certain land. In some cases, all this does is to diminish the concept of marriage into a formal societal arrangement solely to recognize persons under income and tax classifications. In its truest form, a marriage is an understanding between the two people involved and well wishers at large. With that said however, in taking off the superficial social trimmings, the civil registration of a marriage is in place since some of the social laws that pertain to marriage serve to further maintain *societal harmony*. Each couple must decide what is best for them.

Are marriages meant for everyone? The answer is No! In some cultures, there is the great expectation that all persons who reach a certain age are meant to seek out marriages. To persons in such societies, a marriage is compulsory because it is the basis on which they are judged. Sadly, with such practices, many are bound to fall into wrong and loveless marriages because it is simply a fulfillment of that which was imposed upon them by society. *A marriage is not meant for everyone.* It is a personal decision! There are those who are meant to work alone in their earthly journey. These persons might be going against the grain if they seek out a wrong marriage. For you to make the right decision, you must first know yourself well enough to answer this question: Am I meant to work with another so as to fulfill my goals as well as a common unified goal? The answer to this question will determine the path you should take.

In every mature person's life comes a great period that spells a readiness to embark on a journey with another. If the decision is made – naturally and unforced – that it is on one's path to do so, it is exhorted that all persons take conscious steps in enveloping themselves in the truths of living. Only through this do they extricate themselves from living in the shadows of others who have fallen victim to misinformation.

There is nothing more beautiful than a true marriage built on the foundation of true love. Such a union will subsist in absolute and total consonance, joy, and happiness. The concept of a true marriage is synonymous to the workings of an orchestra, in which all instruments, chords, and notes mesh beautifully and harmoniously into the great concinnity and oneness we call music. Oh, what beauty! Such a harmonious union is bound to propel those involved to heights indescribable by mere words, for it transcends all that we as humans are accustomed to seeing. That is the power of love and marriage!

12

LOVE AND HAPPINESS

Whenever the subject of love is at hand, it is almost always associated with the concept of happiness. This is done to a great extent that both words are almost always used in conjunction with each other. As it is, there is the general belief in some circles that if an individual has love he/she is bound to be happy. This has led many to wonder about the connection between love and happiness, if any. Some ponder if we can have one without the other. Which is essentially asking the question: Is one dependent on the other?

In an attempt to address that query, I must pose another question. The purpose of this question is to help readers thoroughly cogitate about the connection between love and happiness. Take a moment to think about this: Should individuals who perceive that love eludes them remain in a state of unhappiness? It is very obvious that no human being is justified in the belief that they should be unhappy because they are not loved. Now, that is not to say that there is no connection between love and happiness, because there is one. However, it is very important to keep in mind that the perceived absence of one of them *should not* determine or negatively affect our emotional state of being, and most importantly, *perception of self.*

THE PURSUIT OF HAPPINESS

As in the case of love, many scurry hither and thither in search of happiness as though true happiness is meant to be pursued. This brings one to ask the question: Was happiness meant to elude the average human being? Well, the answer is an emphatic No! Unfortunately, what many fail to realize is that *true happiness must come from within an individual!* That is saying in essence that true happiness is a feeling that can be achieved and experienced if and only if it comes from the core of one's Being.

Now, it is an irrefutable fact that those who understand the concept of love and are truly loved tend to be happy people. However, in this line of thinking, we must also be aware that the fact that individuals are loved or perceive that they are loved does not automatically bring happiness. This is especially true in the cases of *false love.* The cases of a false perception of happiness happens largely because whatever happiness or euphoria they think they feel is only a figment of their imagination – due to false appearances which are impermanent. These false appearances only provide a limited state of perceived happiness, in which as the pendulum swings, their state of happiness flounders up and down because it is fickle. Thus, it is not true happiness, as *true happiness in creation is everlasting.* As such, the external pursuit or search for happiness is sorely unfounded!

Material possessions can never buy or bring you true happiness. In an attempt to fill a void – which in most cases is self imposed,

some persons focus heavily on the hoarding of earthly possessions or money in the deluded hopes that these material things
will surely bring them complete and unabated happiness, and
perhaps love. While doing this, it is as though they intend to kill
two birds with a stone, in that the money, cars, or houses will automatically provide a passport to the ultimate destination of love
and happiness. Now, there is no doubt that with the right amount
of earthly possessions and tireless public announcements they are
bound to find that which they perceive to be love and happiness.
Well, here is a question to think about: Is the perceived love and
happiness that was gained *only* as a result of their *earthly standing*
real, or is it a facade? The answer should be very obvious. They
may think that the perceived happiness is all real, however, in
actuality, it is all an illusion. Again, let us consider yet another
question: Would their so-called love and happiness remain if all
the material possessions are no more? Well, I think we all know
the answer to that. In most cases, the answer is No.

It must the clarified however that I do not ask these questions
with the intent to clump all materially wealthy persons in the
same category. I am well aware that there are those who have
worked hard and as such have attained a comfortable livelihood
for themselves and their families. I speak of those who tirelessly
and endlessly pursue material things. These are persons who
think that material things present the only passport to the land of
unmitigated appeasement of selfish and meaningless desires –
which they sometimes describe as happiness.

Those who believe that money can buy them love and happiness are in the same boat as those who might foolishly ascribe to
the notion that their money accords them a greater allowance to
breathe in more oxygen than the so-called "poor person." Oxy-

gen, as well as other elements in creation, is free to all earthly inhabitants. To gain access to this gift of nature all you need are functional lungs. No human being is accorded more access to it because of their earthly standing. Such applies to love and happiness! *No human being is accorded more access to true love and happiness because of their earthly standing.*

It should come as no surprise that many of the world's *materially wealthy* people reveal that their earthly possessions do not bring them true happiness; rather, they point to non-materialistic things such as the love of their family and good health. The acquisition and possession of *earthly instruments* such as money, if used rightly, is meant to serve as a tool to achieve and fulfill our *earthly goals*. Sadly, many make the mistake of misappropriating the attainment and achievement of selfish endeavors as the sole determinant of their happiness, and as a result, they entrench themselves in the unending pursuit of superficial things that hold no water in the greater scheme of things.

Now, logically thinking, if the perceived happiness of these persons was defined and determined by their material wealth, it is then only right that they are bound to subsist in an unhappy earthly existence if all their material possessions are taken away due to unforeseen circumstances. I say that because *those who experience true happiness do not depend on material things to make them happy.* The external or material factors only add to their inherent and already existing happiness. What some persons think they feel when in possession of material things is not true happiness – if we judge by the true definition of happiness. Rather, it is a false state of mind which develops into an *illusion of happiness*. Along this line, we must also realize that any human construct that goes against the natural laws of creation will never bring true happiness.

As we commonly witness, there are the many cases of individuals who possess financial wealth but remain extremely empty within. How is that possible? Could it be that they do not have enough to pull them over the happiness threshold? Or does this spell of something greater? In recent times, we have seen the collapse of many of the world systems, which in turn has plunged many individuals once deemed wealthy and prosperous into an instant state of poverty and disillusion. These events are the natural happenings in creation as a sign to mere humans who possess disillusioned grandiose ideas that they have the powers to circumvent natural laws to suit their selfish and materialistic desires. *A structural system that is built on and focuses greatly on materialism with a disinterest in spiritual ascension, basic human morality, and ethical values is bound to fail.* We must realize that the wrong systems enacted by humans will always breed catastrophe and suffering. I bring up this matter because it became apparent that after these events some of the persons affected were able to quickly reconcile the situation and move on, while others were emotional debilitated and damaged by these events. What was the difference between these two parties?

Well, a major difference is that those who were able to move on quickly were those who did not place their material possessions as the sole means or determinant of happiness. To them, the material possessions were simply a means of livelihood and not a tool to promote vanity and ingratiation. Thus, they remain happy and inherently content whether the material persists or not. On the other hand, those who were grossly entrenched in materialism as a means of self-identity and self-worth were emotionally damaged to a point of no return.

I am in no way saying that money and material possessions are useless or that they lack importance. Money is an important part of living. However, we must be mindful that its *sole purpose* is to serve as a tool to enable the trade and exchange of goods and services between people. It has no intrinsic value other than in this physical world. Many qualify this with a saying such as "no one has the ability to utilize money after their death." The money or social status we all attain on earth will never buy us a quick pass or front row seat to everlasting happiness. That simply illustrates that nugatory material valuations have no bearing in the grand scheme of things.

It pains me to see that so many individuals place so much importance on the acquisition of man-made tools, so much so that they tend to forget and sometimes disregard the purpose of their existence here on earth.

THE POTENTIAL OF HAPPINESS IS INHERENT

From our inception into the earth, all earthlings are endowed with the ability to attain and experience true happiness. This ability is indiscriminately granted to all persons. It is there for the taken! What remains a puzzle is that somewhere along the line many lose this inherent potential to be happy. This is largely due to the fact that they entangle themselves with many unnecessary endeavors, which in turn breeds grounds for the continuous outward search for happiness. That then begs the question: Why do so many outwardly pursue that which is inherent within us all?

There are many writers who proclaim to have the answers to *finding* happiness, and most of what they encourage people to do is to build and maintain positive affirmations. Though true in part, positive thoughts and affirmations *alone* will not cut it. What these writers forget to tell or just do not know is that happiness is not something that is meant to be found, because that implies that we are born without it or that it was lost. With that mindset, it is not surprising to see and hear of those who go a lifetime without the absolute feeling of happiness simply because they just could not find it.

The act of outwardly searching for happiness is synonymous to the actions of persons who place their reading glasses on their forehead, and forgetting that they had done so earlier, they search all corners of their premises looking for said glasses; and all this while, that which they tirelessly searched for was in plain sight. To conjure up the happiness within, we must rid ourselves of all that is material. That is to say that we must remove all material considerations in assessing happiness. True happiness can only come through *spiritual wealth*. It is open to those who are "rich in spirit." *The happiest persons are those who uphold the highest spiritual standard of living.*

THE DEFINITION OF TRUE HAPPINESS

True Happiness is a state of being in which one is whole. This wholeness comes as a result of a greater sense of self-awareness and contentment. It could also help to think of happiness as an inherent feeling that comes with being at one with nature. The contentment and self-awareness that is emblematic of true happiness is largely due to the fact that individuals are mindful of their *purpose in creation* and that they consciously strive to enact it. An important indicator of happiness is self-love and contentment. People who truly love themselves are bound to be happy. *True love of oneself presents a direct passage to long-lasting happiness.*

Another major correlation between the concepts of love and happiness is that *true love can only serve to foster happiness*. It is undoubtedly true that the concepts of love and happiness come to play when many talk about their relationships with family members, friends, and a marital partner. And as we all know, most tend to place more focus on marital partnerships. On that account, it is important to note that true love should only enhance the happiness and contentment you should inherently feel. So, in essence, the existence of love in your life should only add to your already existing happiness, and not as the sole source for happiness.

It is a grave mistake to depend on the love or affection from another as the sole source of one's happiness. If you expect to gain happiness from wrong relationships, you will most certainly be disappointed. If you depend solely on the love and affection from others to determine your happiness, you must also be ready to wallow in unhappiness if the perceived love comes to a cessation. The love and grace to fulfill as humans should give every individual the greatest feeling of joy and happiness, while the love we receive from others should come only as an addendum to that which we already feel. In so speaking, when we look at unions and partnerships, we must keep in mind that the right relationships should only further strengthen the happiness that one was meant to inherently possess. If the love one professes to feel for another does not help to maintain and foster happiness, then they must reassess their engagement in such a relationship. One of the conditions of true love is that it can only serve to bring happiness to those involved. Therefore, anything in opposition of happiness should not be misconstrued as love, because *true love can never encourage negative feelings*.

True happiness dwells in children. It is no coincidence that most children are very happy. The major reason for this is that they have not been introduced to the frivolities of material pursuits. As such, they remain at a state which is closer to the spiritual realm. Some might assume that they are not yet *conscious of self* therefore they have no concept of true happiness. That is not true! Every Being is born with a sense of consciousness. Though it is true that the conscious state of a child is not yet fully developed, it does exist. There should be no reason why many assume that "maturity" means that they must clog their minds, and as such, must only think of *mature things*. Why must we run away from childlikeness in an attempt to prove maturity? In the attempts to engage in these so-called "mature acts" all we tend to do is strive further and further away from true happiness.

True happiness lies in simplicity. In order to be truly at peace and happy, you must learn to be simple, humble, and childlike. You must allow the happiness within you to unfold. How do you do that? Simple! You accomplish that by engaging in positive activities that foster true happiness. Everyone is born with unique abilities that will enable them to add to the betterment of humanity. If you do that which you are cut-out to do, you are bound to be happy. Only in living in accordance with the natural laws of creation will one tread the path to true happiness.

For those who remain in a constant state of unhappiness, please remember: You hold the key to your happiness. Now, you must proactively unlock the happiness that dwells within. The message is simple: Be happy!

13

LOVE OF A CHILD

When should the love and preparation of a child truly begin? Some individuals think that the preparation and love of a child should commence at the point of conception, while others believe that the love of a child begins when the child is born anew. Are those who hold these different opinions and beliefs wrong? Well, the answer is No! They are all right in the sense that the love of a child must begin very early and should continue through that child's lifespan. But the real question I am driving at is: How early should the love of a child begin?

Those who hold varying opinions on this topic possess grains of truth. The point of this discussion is not to discount the validity and expertise of those in the medical sciences who provide helpful advice to their patients on when to begin child care. The point of this discussion is to clearly state that *the love of a child should begin before the point of conception of the child*. And this should begin a *long time* before the process leading to conception even commences. I am sure that this might sound like a new idea or concept to some people, however nothing that I speak of is new.

From the beginning of our existence, there was a grand plan enacted by the Creator, in which the ability by earthlings to procreate was a grace given to humankind to help further the works that need to be completed. Therefore, if there was an original plan for our existence, it is only logical that there should be a grand plan in our activities to procreate.

THE CURRENT STATE OF THE WORLD

In many parts of the world, it is almost commonplace to turn on the television and expect an advertisement from an international charity group appealing to the masses to donate all they can to help in providing aid to a suffering and deprived child some place in the world. What is more appalling is that such announcements have become so prevalent that we are sometimes immune to them. It is almost as though they are now expected. The need for such help gives rise to an important question: Why should such be the case? Now, it is a commendable feat that we all gather and try to help each other in a time of need. However, are we really helping or making matters worse? It will be more helpful if we try to assess the root of the problem, with the hopes that in addressing the root of the problem we in turn might have the best solution to deal with such problems. Though it is natural for humans to want to help in such cases, we must realize that what these individuals truly need is the *education in understanding what true love of a child truly entails.*

A major reason for the suffering of so many children stems from the meaningless actions of experimenters who engage in acts of which they lack full maturity and knowledge, for they simply do not understand the seriousness of what they are doing. It is hard to conceptualize the logic or rationale in the minds of those who engage in intercourse, sometimes with unknown persons, which in turn create the possibility of pregnancy. And as a result, they become pregnant in cases now comfortably dubbed "unplanned pregnancies" and "teenage pregnancies." Unfortunately, due to the prevalence of such cases, some individuals now perceive these occurrences to be acceptable, as it is deemed "all a part of living as a human being." What we tend to forget is that these actions do not denote love of self, and consequently, love of a child.

As it is, due to the misguidance of some persons, it is now commonplace for males to question the paternity of a child. And as if that is not bad enough, in most of these cases, the females themselves are also unsure who the father of their child is. What a disgrace! This has now given rise to the immense popularity of "DNA tests." In scenes reminiscent of dungeon-like activities, many now appear on public forums to debate and fight over the paternity of a child. In these nationally televised programs, many of these individuals are encouraged to stupidly parade around as they judge their cases to a patronizing audience. As it is, the paternity of a child is now a public forum debate open for all to chime in. Do we not see that something is wrong with this picture? Do these actions denote true love of a child? It pains me to say that these actions greatly illustrate the *decay of human society*.

Does the fact that we are human beings mean that we lack the ability to reason and formulate rationale in all our actions? Or does being human imply that we are bound to act without logic or rationale? The birth of a child into the physical world is a matter of great importance and must not be taken lightly. Sadly, what we see today are the overwhelming cases of individuals who take such matters lightly, as evident in the actions of some adults and youngsters who unashamedly engage in deeds that illustrate self-hatred and self-abuse; and at the end, a child is to be born. How unfortunate! No child should ever be called an "orphan" or labeled a "mistake." It is unnatural and unfair that a child is subjected to such!

BRINGING A CHILD INTO THIS WORLD

In looking at the world population and the expected growth in the coming years, it is very apparent that in most cases the adequate planning and preparation for the coming of a child is not practiced. This in turn has led to the great suffering of many newborn spirits who are subject to living in adjunct poverty, of which, in essence, they have no future. Can this be averted? Well, the answer is Yes! Now, in saying that, I do not intend to mislead anyone into thinking that the planning and preparation for the coming of a child would automatically obviate the child from suffering or being subjected to a state of poverty, as there are many spirits that have great karmas that must be rectified at a new birth. However, in planning and preparing for the coming of a child, the parents of said child have proven that they are spiritually, mentally, physically, emotionally, and materially equipped to help nurture this child into becoming a positive contributor of the world. *True love of a child entails that both parents prepare the grounds for the child's arrival.* Both parties must have a common reason and rationale as to their purpose for attempting to bring a child into this world. Their reasons must be pure!

The reasons to bring a child into this world must not stem from the unconscious actions of individuals in matters which they know nothing about. This refers to the many cases of youngsters who engage in acts that are meant for emotionally and physically mature persons. Engaging in such acts only serves to put them in the predicament of having to become adults overnight. It is practically a case of *children bearing children*. It would behoove these individuals to know that *bringing a child into this world is no child's play*.

The reasons to commence actions to bring a child into this world should not stem from the superficial desires of humans to populate a land. As it is, in some parts of the world, some individuals attempt to bring children into this world based on the results of scientific studies that point to a decline in human population growth; in which case, there is a great demand or market for new people to be brought into the world simply to aid the future workforce. These happenings greatly diminish the importance of the birth of a child into a silly game of supply and demand. That must stop!

The reason for bringing a child into this world must not be an obligatory action solely due to the fact that two persons are married. The actions must not be taken so as to appease others who expect or anticipate the birth of a child, as some believe that it is only natural to attempt to give birth to a child when individuals are deemed to be in love. The fact that two persons are married or in a committed relationship does not implicitly mean that they are meant to bear children. Doing so without absolute conviction in their actions puts them in a condition in which they allow others to dictate their destiny. Such allowance is injudicious!

We should not attempt to bring a child into this world solely on the basis of selfish desires to proliferate and aid the continuance of a family lineage by the adoption of a surname or last name. In some cultures, it is deemed a great achievement to give birth to a male child, while female children are essentially treated as second class citizens in their families – as they are deemed practically invaluable. What a disgrace to humanity! There are the many cases in which a woman is not respected or valued simply because she has only given birth to female children. As a result, there is the unending chase to give birth to a male child by all means possible. This desire leads many women into selling their souls in the great pursuit of a male child. Even worse, it is sometimes advised that husbands procure more wives in the hopes that this might increase the chances that a male child will magically appear in the family. Thus, the woman who accomplishes this feat is greatly respected by other family members as though she has done something great. What a shame! Though some of these practices are changing as many have become aware of the silliness of such behavior, sadly, they still occur in certain parts of the world.

A CONSCIOUS DECISION

The need to give birth to a child should be a conscious *decision*. This decision should come as a result of a thorough and unswerving conviction that both individuals must tread on that path. The word "decision" is emphasized to illustrate that *true love of a child requires the meeting of minds of both parents, in which they both consciously and knowingly agree to take the necessary steps to procreate.* This decision

must stem from the fact that both parties are spiritually, mentally, physically, emotionally, and materially ready to bear the responsibility to care, nurture, and guide a child to full maturity.
Due to the current state of our world, such preparedness is imperative.

Ideally, the preparation for the coming of a new spirit into the physical world should begin long before married persons engage in the act that would spark such a possibility. The immense love for a child would demand that they plan and prepare for the coming of the child. In so doing they would lay the grounds for the smooth arrival of this new Being into the physical world.

True love of a child demands that parents love themselves first. Only then can they truly transpose love to a child. As we know by now, it is impossible to claim to love another if we don't love ourselves, because the actions taken will be done under the premise of misguided beliefs of love, which in most cases are in opposition to the principles of true love. Therefore the love of a child necessitates that parents know and love themselves first. In no greater instance is it more apparent to love ourselves as it is in the case in which we are now responsible for the upbringing of a new Being. We must realize that the fact that an individual possesses the physical ability to procreate does not automatically mean that he/she is meant to do so or that they are destined to give birth to a child.

Now, if parents consciously decide to take the steps to bring a new spirit into the physical world, where do they go from there? There are those who strongly believe that they had no direct decision in choosing their parents, and parents sometimes make similar claims about their children. Interestingly, some parents and children sometimes joke that if they had the choice they would have chosen other persons. Well, to fight such a mindset, those who make such complaints must realize that the *child-parent dynamic is a 50/50 partnership*. That is to say that no party has the justification to blame the other. The parents simply provided the platform, and the child chose the opportunity to experience. The fact that parents took the necessary steps to open up the doors to the physical realm of experiencing for their children is direct proof that the relationship from its inception was destined in order to allow both parties to experience and grow. Therefore, the complaints from either side are invalid and unfounded. Parents should not blame their children; likewise, no child should blame his/her parents. Both parties are equally responsible. In saying that however, it is important to keep in mind that the parents hold a greater level of responsibility during the formative years of a child, as they must provide the necessary tools to enable this child to become what he/she was meant to be.

It is true that parents cannot directly hand-pick their children. However, the measures taken before pregnancy, during pregnancy, and after pregnancy play a great and unmistakable role in the types of children they bring on earth. Medically, it is a fact that those who engage in frivolities during pregnancy run a greater risk of giving birth to a child with physical and mental complications. Therefore, the love of a child necessitates that parents take all *precautions known to humans* in the hopes that they will be blessed with a child who is healthy and free of ailments at new birth. To achieve this, both parties must purify their bodies. However, this purification goes much deeper than the physical. It must also come with the cleansing and refinement of their thoughts, words, and deeds – so as to open the doors for *light spirits*.

Love of a child demands that parents have taken steps to prove that they can provide adequate care to nurture a child. There are those who perceive that just by providing the material needs of their children they qualify as "good parents." In some cases, this meaningless provision of material needs is done as though they are doing their children a huge favor. The prevalence of such cases in certain societies of the world has led to the referencing and naming of these individuals as "deadbeat parents." The overwhelming occurrence of these cases has led many to assume that providing for their children is a "choice" and not an "obligation." Consequently, those who provide for their children due to a mandate from a governmental agency now believe that they deserve meritorious labels. What a shame! It would behoove these persons to know that true love of a child comes in many dimensions. Though the provision of material things is needed and commendable, it is only a small portion of the total picture. In addition to the material provisions, they must also provide spiritual, emotional, and mental support. These are the most important aspects.

Now, by the same token, there are those who believe that showering and "spoiling" their children with material gifts – as though they intend to buy the child's love and affection – demonstrates that they love that child. Such behavior is unadvised! Providing a child with all material *desires* rather than *needs* is bound to create indolence and laxity in that child. We see the manifestation of such in the many cases in which a child essentially becomes a menace to those around them simply because their parents have allowed them to believe that they are *entitled* to whatever they desire; at which point the word "No" is nonexistent in their frame of consciousness. Parents must teach and raise their children to become aware of their limitations. And this should be done with the teachings that the earth maintains a balance, as such, it is only logical that all persons must also maintain a balance and not indulge in excesses.

On the opposite spectrum, there are those who absolutely relinquish and sign-off the responsibilities of care for a child solely to the other parent. While in the same boat, there are those who frolic around by seeking thrills, and in doing so they impregnate multiply females, of which as a result, they are now so-called "fathers" to many children, of whom they cannot cater for. Even worse, in most cases, these persons cannot even cater for themselves. Likewise, there are the females who hop from male to male and in so doing procure many children. These persons are not fit to be called parents or even respected as such. There seems to be a great disengagement in the mode of thinking of these individuals. And this disengagement is as a result of their lack of consciousness that engaging in the act that can lead to pregnancy requires that they must be ready to bear the consequences.

Some unpropitious experiences await those who have the impudence to give birth with the hopes that another will be responsible for their child's upbringing. The sole responsibility to rear a child lies with the parents of said child. The support from family members or friends should only come as an added help, not the primary consideration. It will behoove these individuals to know that if they are not ready for the immense responsible of a child, it is then only judicious that they *abstain from acts that can spark such possibilities.* Now, to some of these persons, this notion might sound like an unknown or foreign language that is hard to comprehend, as they are greatly materialistic and must seek meaningless physical thrills at all cost. But, for those who can still hear the message, it is advised that they wake up from their deep slumber and tread aright. The act that can lead to the conception and pregnancy of a child is meant for those who are spiritually, mentally, physically, and emotionally mature. Thus, they are ready, equipped, and willing to take on the responsible that will ensue as a result of the arrival of the newcomer – the child.

Now, other than the necessary self-analysis in thoroughly assessing if one is ready to procreate, a major step in ensuring that we open the doors for the arrival of good spirits is in making sure that the decision to bear children is done with one's true and destined partner. It is bewildering to notice that some individuals have become comfortable with the labels "Baby Mama" or "Baby Daddy." As it is, there is a puzzling laxity in the utterance of these words. It is almost as though such existence should be a normal occurrence in human living – which it shouldn't.

In looking at the state of the world, it is all too apparent that so many who bear children today do so with individuals with whom they were probably not supposed to. This in turn gives rise to the many instances in which children are raised by one parent. Now, in saying that, I must clarify that I do not intend to give the impression that single parents lack the capacity to love their children as married or committed couples do, because in *some cases* most children are better off being brought up by one parent who will guide them on the right path. With that said however, in order to mitigate the likelihood of unwarranted experiences by bearing a child with the wrong partner, you must first know yourself. Thus, you are in charge of your destiny. Being in charge of your destiny, you are bound to make better decisions.

HOW TO LOVE A CHILD

True Love of a child demands that all parents are proactive in the rearing and upbringing of a child. As I mentioned earlier, the proactiveness in the rearing of a child must start long before the arrival of the new Being. Both parents should be active participants in the rearing and upbringing of a child. Nothing can substitute for the love of a parent; as it can be a great gift in pushing a child to achieve beyond bounds. The upbringing of a child is the greatest determinant of how that child will turn out. Those who are fortunate to experience the right upbringing and true love from a parent – not false love shrouded in indulgent behavior – are more focused in their endeavors and goals in life. That should tell us the importance of the right upbringing.

True love of a child demands that parents must teach children how to effectively love themselves. Those who love themselves are those who strive to live positive lifestyles! As we know by now, the love of oneself is a great determinant in how we interact with others, and it is undoubtedly true that an individual's perception of self is primordially derived from their parents. To further elucidate on this point, a male child who has learned the true meaning of love from his mother will only grow to expect the utmost from a potential marital partner. The same logic goes for a female child who has an upstanding male figure.

Children must be thought to respect themselves as well as others. As we have learned, only those who love and respect themselves will be able to transpose such to others. Therefore, it is imperative that children are brought up to respect their parents; likewise, parents should also respect their children. Parents must realize that respect is reciprocal. It must be given to be received.

Needless to say, no child-parent relationship will exist harmoniously without a healthy respect on both sides. That tells us the importance of mutual respect.

True Love of a child demands that parents must act as the ideal role models to their children. It is painfully apparent that many parents just do not understand the great influence they have on their children; and as a result, they set the wrong examples for them to follow. It is a sad state to see that many children look to outside figures as their ideal role models. Now, there is nothing wrong with the admiration of others whom they feel have qualities that are exemplary of what they would like to be – especially in the case of a profession. But, unfortunately, in some cases, these outside role models are essentially substituted in the place of a parent. That should not be the case! Parents must not relegate their duties to outsiders. Granted, there are outsiders – teachers, mentors, or friends – who will help in shaping a child, however, the primary responsibilities belong to the parents.

In the ideal circumstances, parents are meant to be the ideal role models to their children. This is done when there is strict alignment in what they teach and how they act. A parent is one who is meant to inculcate and instill the necessary values in a child. Now, it is important to note that in order to be able to effectively bestir one's child in the right direction, one must first be aware of these values. Giving allowance to a child to freely roam without guidance is sorely unadvised. It is therefore admonished that those who intend to be parents must first establish a self-identity. They must know who they are, and most importantly, what they stand for. They must remain unswervingly strong in absolute conviction of their beliefs. As a sidebar however, these beliefs must be in alignment with natural laws. Any ideas or beliefs that are in opposition to the natural laws and principles at play in creation are bound to create more confusion and suffering.

It is advised that parents set the right foundations and examples for their children. Only in doing so will a child be accorded the opportunity to learn and grow aright. It is hypocritical to tell a child to *"do as I say, not as I do."* Such a statement only exposes the true weaknesses of the parents. All things being right, *parents should live what they preach.* Their actions and words must be in strict alignment. They should not contradict themselves. Consider this: *If all parents stand aright, no child will fall!*

True love of a child demands that parents protect their children from that which their eyes must not see and that which their ears must not hear. It is clear that we are at an age in which anyone can easily gain access to any type of information, and those more susceptible to the easy availability of such information are children. Therefore, parents must proactively take all necessary measures to protect their children. They must ensure that children are only allowed to see, hear, and say things that are appropriate. As we all know, there are many stages in life and the skipping of stages is bound to make a child grow up prematurely, and a child who grows up prematurely is more inclined to make errors in judgment.

Naturally, children are bound to mature as they grow older, so why hasten the process? Nature necessitates that a fruit must be ripened for it to provide the needed nutrients and nourishment, if not, it is innutritious and sour to the taste. This logic greatly applies to human beings, in that a child must reach full maturity before he/she is allowed to experience freely. Any allowance for misguided and destructive behavior before full maturity will only bring *sour results.*

Before children come to an age when they can freely experience and make important decisions from their own volition, parents remain responsible and accountable for the deeds of their children. In some societies, there is a strong debate on how to trial children who commit grievous crimes. Some exhort and support that such children are prosecuted as adults, while others believe that they should be judged as children – due to their age. Now, in all these arguments, we forget to ask ourselves the all important question: What role did that child's parents play in their action? By this, I do not ask if the parents were physical participants in the deed, encouraged, or were present during the act. No, that is not what I am getting at! What I am asking in essence pertains to the *upbringing* of such a child. Did the parents of this child instill the right values in him? Or did they indulge destructive behavior at home, which essentially leads the child to believe that such behavior has no bounds and can be exhibited to outsiders?

Sadly, as it is, there are those who rear their children to believe that it is within their right to be destructive if they do not get their way. In these cases, why should we be surprised when a child takes up arms and proceeds to harm others if they do not get things their way? With that said, we must realize that *parents hold some responsibility for the destructive actions of their children before adulthood.* It is highly improbable that a child raised with the right values would consciously engage in destructive behavior. Therefore, it is exhorted that parents create boundaries for their children. Parents must not be enablers. A child without boundaries is bound to be a peril to himself, and worse, to humanity at large.

True love of a child is embodied by the utmost level of discipline. In nature there are checks and balances, it is therefore necessary that parents must play a balancing role for their children. That is to say that truly loving a child demands that parents must provide the necessary discipline to help guide the child. When a child goes astray, it is the responsibility and duty of the parents to steer the child back on the right path. *Parents must not encourage indolence in any child!* Doing so can only breed laxity of the body, mind, and soul. Although some children might object at first, it is amazing to see that a huge number of adults admire and praise their parents for providing them with a disciplined lifestyle when they were youngsters. For many, this revelation comes as a result of the values instilled in them from a young age, which has aided them to be focused individuals in adulthood.

True love of a child demands that parents know their children. Each child is unique. Thus he/she will possess unique and special traits. So it is the responsibility of parents to become aware of the strengths and weaknesses of a child. In knowing the potentials of a child, it is much easier to help the child. There are some children who have the tendency to be stubborn, for these children certain disciplinary methods might be ineffective. And the continuance of such methods in the hopes of instilling discipline will be to no avail. Even worse, these disciplinary methods might serve to hurt or harm rather than help the child. The acknowledgement of a child's weaknesses and strengths will help parents steer the child in the right directions. Parents must help nurture the strengths of a child and work on the weaknesses.

True love of a child demands that parents do not "kill" a child's talents and aspirations in an attempt to suit their own selfish desires and needs. The emphasis on the word "kill" is meant to draw attention to the acts of those who overly encourage, and in some cases, create a mandate as to what professions their children must adapt. This is in essence killing the child! Parents must allow children to exhibit and enact the natural talents and abilities they possess. This talent was given for a specific purpose and *must not be squelched to gear them into things they are not naturally gifted to do.*

Though in most cases the encouragement and push from parents come as a result of love and concern for the welfare of the child, it does not serve to help the child unfold and fulfill naturally. Due to the squelching of their true talents, we get to see the cases of many persons who are engaged in careers that do not provide them any sense of fulfillment or purpose. Consider a child who possesses artistic abilities from an early age but the parents think that the artistic ability will not provide a lucrative lifestyle for the child when he/she becomes an adult. And with that mindset, they decide to gear all the child's education and training towards being a physician – as that is deemed to be a more lucrative and respectable profession. Now, the thought in itself is not wrong because it comes from a good place. However, if as a physician this individual now goes into a deep depression because he/she was just not cut-out to be a physician, it is sad to say that the parents are partly responsible for that. This child was a born artist and it was the responsibility of the parents to help nurture the child along that line. Parents must provide the necessary guidance, however they must not go against the natural ordinance.

Now, with that said, it is important to note that although it is advised that parents should allow their children to unfold, they should not allow them to wallow aimlessly in *unproductive endeavors* under the guise of discovering themselves. Rather, parents must nurture a child's abilities and talents, so that when they become of age they can make a decision as to the path they want to follow. Children must be thought that they are in existence for a purpose and must strive to discover that purpose.

It is unadvised that parents turn their children into money-making puppets. Doing so can only lead a child down the path of becoming an adult before they were truly meant to. That does not help a child! *A child must be given the opportunity to naturally grow into adulthood, and not forced into it.* In the ideal conditions, those who plan to be parents must have taken conscious steps and measures to ensure that they can provide the needed support for their children. With the proper planning, there will be no need to put a child into gainful employment so as to aid, or in some cases, become the main source of support for their parents. Now, many might also wonder about the cases of "child prodigies" who exude strong talents in certain areas. Well, in those cases, it is the responsibility of the parent to help nurture this talent until the child is of age to make a conscious decision for himself.

In view of what we have touched on thus far, it is easy to see that true love of a child is bound to exalt the parents as well as the child. The greatest gift any parent can give a child is true love. A truly loved child is bound to become a gift to humanity. Please remember: Never forget to love a child!

14

THE VOICE OF LOVE

The voice of love speaks to the consciousness of humanity. It resounds at the highest frequencies known to human beings. This voice shall not speak to the ears so as to be disseminated by the eardrums; rather, it shall speak to the core of all conscious persons.

The voice of love speaks to the heart. It is a voice that will be felt; for it speaks loudly and clearly to all who are ready to listen. This voice shall speak so profoundly that it will penetrate through the most hardened skeptic. It shall impel all conscious persons into a heightened state of awareness.

The voice of love shall speak of what love was meant to be in creation. Through this voice many are bound to know the essence of true love. In listening to this voice, many will come to the realization that we are all a product of love in creation. Thus we must live every moment of our earthly existence in the light of love.

The voice of love shall define love for all to understand. This voice speaks to all conscious persons who have not relinquished their abilities to see what truly is. It does not ascribe to a system of thought that lacks logic. It will speak to those who strive for enlightenment. This voice shall awake all to the realities around them. It shall bring forth an enlightenment that will propel many into a heightened spiritual standard of living.

The voice of love is trustworthy, compassionate, forgiving, honest, respectful, supportive, committed, loyal, altruistic, patient, caring, responsible, accountable, and truthful. This voice encourages all to pay attention to the inherent virtues of humanity. It tells that love in its truest form is severe; and in understanding the severity of love, many are bound to set themselves free.

The voice of love implores all conscious persons to stop the blind pursuit of love. This voice tells all that in the pursuit of love you must never lose sight of who you are. You must not allow yourself to become a dispensable filler in the pleasure seeking thrills of another. This voice exhorts that all conscious persons must take themselves out of the shadows of self-enslavement. It encourages all not to look for love, but to seek relationships that are defined by true love. If asked: How is your love life? This voice encourages all to answer with confidence: *"My love life is full."* Love is everywhere, love is in everyone, love is the ability to wake up every morning, love is in the air you breathe, love is the gift of sight, love is in silence, love is in nature, and much more. Simply put, love is in all we perceive in creation. Love in creation is infinite.

The voice of love speaks of true love of self. It tells all that true love of self can only come from within. It encourages all persons to be inherently aware of their self-worth. This voice teaches all that loving thyself means that you respect and value yourself. It advises that in order to love thy neighbor, you must first love yourself. Simply put, you must do unto thy neighbor what you want done unto you! In order to truly love thyself you must be in tune with your inner self; for if you are in tune with yourself, the voice of love will speak to your spirit. This voice will shake the spirit to awaken from its slumber; for if the spirit is awakened, it will relay the right messages. It will act as a guide in all you think, say, and do. Through the voice of love many are bound to know the true definition of self-love.

The voice of love shall make many aware of the gross laxity in the use of words. It tells that freedom of speech does not mean that we can spew out words which we do not mean or even understand. Words are meant to convey the messages of our true feelings. Thus, if uttered, they must be meaningful. We must use our words wisely. This voice tells all that the adherence to doctrines that hold no logic will create more suffering than exaltation. The voice of love does not appeal to the sensibilities of humans. It does not sway to the drumbeats of popular culture or the latest fad. It is not a partial voice, nor does it hold any biases. Irrespectively, it speaks the truth.

The voice of love implores all conscious persons to purify their thoughts, words, and actions. This voice exhorts all to think, speak, and act with absolute conviction and consciousness. This voice shall speak through the conscience of conscious persons. It tells that the wrong behaviors of humanity shall manifest as *conscience pangs*. It tells that only those who act aright will be at ease with their conscience. Hence we must awaken our conscience. The conscience speaks to humans whether or not they are aware of its existence. It tells all to listen to the little voice. Though silent, it speaks volume. Though little, it speaks loudly and profoundly. Please listen and you shall hear it!

The voice of love shall spell out the conditions of love. Through this voice many will come to know that love can never be defined by suffering. True love is ennoblement. This voice shall speak to those who are ready for a change. It shall speak to those who inherently know what is right but do not have the will and fortitude to make the necessary changes in their lives. It shall act as a guide to all who desire to follow the path originally intended for humanity.

The voice of love shall advice all that the drive for physical gratification will never lead to fulfillment. Lust resides on the surface. The attraction to a body part will only get you just that. It will only get you a body part. Through this voice most will come to the realization that they must seek and follow an attraction of the spirit. With an attraction of the spirit, they shall get to experience true love of the highest order.

The voice of love tells that the only way to live in consonance is through utmost compatibility. It spells out the keys to a truly harmonious union – the scale of compatibility. This voice advises all persons that without spiritual, mental, and physical compatibility no relationship can stand aright. It tells that without these components in place a relationship or union will not rise to see the morning light, as it is bound to die in the darkness of the night.

The voice of love encourages all persons to seek love-defined unions. We must do this with the awareness that a true marriage can only grow to be solidified with love as its foundation. This voice encourages all to grow in love rather than fall in love. In growing there is room for improvement. When we fall, it is difficult to maintain a balanced stance. As in nature, more so in the matters of love, growth connotes a constant and steadfast journey to maturity. When we grow, we mature! Through this voice many shall come to the realization that a marriage or union built on the foundation of true love will propel all parties involved to heights yet unknown by humans.

The voice of love speaks of true happiness. It tells all that true happiness lies in simplicity. Through this voice all of humanity shall come to the realization that the happiest persons are those who uphold the highest spiritual standard of living. Happiness is everywhere. Only you can conjure up the inherent happiness endowed in you. You must allow this happiness to unfold. Give your happiness free rein to blossom. Be happy!

The voice of love implores all to love their children. Parents and custodians must impart in their children the teachings of self-love. This voice tells that no child should ever be labeled or stigmatized as an orphan. One of the keys to unlocking the possibilities for humanity lies in truly loving a child. A child who is truly loved has the potential of becoming a blessing to humanity.

The voice of love speaks of the great possibilities that await humanity – a new norm. Through this voice many shall become aware of a new way of living. This new way of living is the way of love. This voice speaks of a time when all of humanity will come to know what true love stands for. Through this voice many will come to know the standard of true love.

The voice of love knows no limitations. It does not recognize human-made blockades. It shall promulgate a message that will break through all geographic, cultural, and personal barriers. It shall speak to all persons irrespective of their earthly location. This voice does not heed to fables. It does not spew out rhetoric; rather, it speaks with clarity. It shall speak a language that all persons will understand – the language of love. This voice will bore through all corners of the earth, because it shall travel at the speed of an ethereal thought. This is a speed immeasurable by earthlings. Through this voice all of humanity will come to know the universal truths and principles of love.

The voice of love is the voice of truth and reason. This voice shall speak to the many persons who seek answers but know not where to find them. It knows that although some might object to its teachings, deep down they are aware that it speaks the truth. It shall speak to those who have a great yearning for the truth, as it is bound to bring to light that which the darkness has tried to conceal. This voice shall make all conscious persons rejoice, for the truths of love have been finally unveiled to humanity.

Listen! Please listen carefully as the voice of love speaks! Why should you listen? Well, you should listen because the voice of love is within you. It is the voice within that speaks to you. The voice of love is your voice. *Love is the confluence of all that is good within you.* Now, let your love shine forth!

THIS IS MY MESSAGE

I understand that it is only natural to wonder about the origin or the identity of the author of this work; however, I would like to say that the identity of the messenger is not important. What is of utmost relevance is the message itself. The messenger only serves as a medium in rendering a much needed service to humanity; such as doctors would do for their patients or as teachers would do for their pupils. My work is no greater than theirs!

There are those destined to bring forth or retell the truths in creation to humanity, and seeking fame in doing such works can sometimes take away the attention of the audience from the message, as we have seen in countless cases. So readers should focus intently on the message rather than engaging in extensive research or investigations as to the identity of the messenger. The message is what counts!

The intent of this work is not to bring about a new "love religion" or to convert readers into mindless and thoughtless followers of the words; rather, it is to foment conscious thought in persons who will find logic in the words presented. It is my hope that this work will unclog the ears of those who have not yet heard the truths of love. The ultimate goal is to bring the lore of love to the universal mainstream.

My greatest hope and desire is that all seekers who come across this work will entrench themselves in the lore of the truth, thus awakening to a greater consciousness of what love was meant to be for humankind. I also hope that all those who have gained something valuable from this book will recommend it to others who might also find it helpful.

I do not say that adhering to all the principles contained in this book will bring instant happiness and immediately obviate one from suffering. It will be unwise to think that way, as there are other facets of living that might need to be addressed before one can achieve that feat. However, what I can say with absolute confidence is that the knowledge and conscious application of the principles entailed in this book will be a great leap forward.

For those who do not find logic in the message presented in this work, they are hereby *free* to continue on the path they deem fit for themselves. However, if that path leads to suffering, confusion, and self-enslavement in the name of love, it is my hope that they will consciously reevaluate the path they choose to follow.

I envisage a world in which all inhabitants of the earth will move at the speed of love. I envisage a world in which all actions, thoughts, and words will be driven by true love. I envisage a world in which all persons will hold themselves to the highest standard of love. Oh, the possibilities! This great possibility for humanity spells a "New Norm." This new norm spells that humanity is ripe for a transformation. The new norm is within reach, all we have to do is to let it be.

I do not seek fame or adoration by making this work available to the world. The only form of gratification I hope to get is an emotional remuneration. My sense of fulfillment will be heightened because I am aware that at any given time somewhere in the world someone who has read this work will henceforth live in the light of love. That will make my efforts worthwhile, for this work was truly a labor of love.

It is my fervent hope that this work will live on to prosperity; for works that tell the truth never die. The truth is timeless. The truth will remain for eons. It will quench the thirst and yearning for knowledge time and time again. It is my hope that through this work many will come to the realization that the standard of love is of the highest order, for herein lies the definitive manifesto of what true love should be.

This pronouncement is to humanity
The scales fall from the eyes
And human beings are enabled to see again
There is now no point to search hither and thither
Humans must not live in a veil of mendacity
We must obviate ourselves from a nescient existence
The Truth is near
All humanity has to do is grasp it
Now strive forward with lore
When love is light
Why live in darkness
We must live in the light of love!

PUBLISHER'S NOTE

At J. Skylimit Publishing, we appreciate your feedback, comments, or questions. For bulk orders of this book or to write the author, please send all inquiries to:

J. Skylimit Publishing
P.O. Box 649
South Pasadena, California 91031

OR

To contact the author by email, please send messages to:
Bjjerremy@gmail.com

Thank you!

www.ingramcontent.com/pod-product-compliance
Lightning Source LLC
LaVergne TN
LVHW011347080426
835511LV00005B/173